D1165215

THE ILLUSTRATED HISTORY OF THE
SUBMARINE

Edward Horton

THE ILLUSTRATED HISTORY OF THE
SUBMARINE

Edward Horton

Doubleday & Company, Inc.
Garden City, New York

43435 2/75 DD 10.00

Made and Printed in Great Britain

Copyright © 1974 Edward Horton and Sidgwick and Jackson Limited

Design by Bob Burroughs

ISBN 0 385 05614-1

Library of Congress
Catalog Card Number
9406989

Below: In December 1952 this German midget submarine was found buried in a sand beach near Amsterdam. Ten years earlier the midget's big brother, the U-boat, had waged a ferocious struggle for mastery of the north Atlantic

Previous page: Morning exercises on a Russian Pacific Fleet submarine in 1955

Contents

ACKNOWLEDGEMENTS

Associated Press Ltd 114–115

British Museum/photo RB Fleming © Sidgwick & Jackson 11, 18–19, 23, 26–27 (bottom), 28–29, 42–43, 50–51 (top), 52–53, 62–63 (middle)

British Museum/Science Museum photo 38–39, 58–59, 134–135

Bur. Mar. Hist. v.d. Marinestaf, Holland 13 (top and both middle)

Camera Press Ltd 153 (top), 154, 158

Foto Drüppel, Wilhelmshaven 62–63 (top), 98 (top & bottom), 112–113, 113

Fox Photos Ltd 109 (middle), 157 (top)

General Dynamics, Electric Boat Division 17, 148–149, 153 (bottom) 155, 159

Imperial War Museum 60–61, 62–63 (bottom), 64–65 (top), 66–67 (top), 73, 75 (top), 76–77, 78, 84, 85, 98, 98–99, 104–105, 106–107, 107, 109, 110, 126, 128–129, 131 (top & middle), 132, 133, 134, 135, 136–137, 140–141 (top), 146–147, 151

Keystone Press Agency 4–5, 34–35 (top), 156 (top & bottom)

Mansell Collection 13 (bottom), 14–15, 18, 44–45 (bottom), 57

Marcus Hinton Collection 94 (middle & bottom)

J. G. Moore 34–35 (bottom), 48–49, 79 (bottom), 80, 81, 83, 87, 93, 97

Musée de la Marine, Paris 30–31, 44–45 (top), 50–51 (bottom)

National Portrait Gallery 20

Novosti Press Agency 2, 124–125

Popperfoto Ltd 140–141

Radio Times Hulton Picture Library 94 (top)

Submarine Force Library & Museum, Connecticut 33, 46–47, 142

Süddeutscher Verlag, Munich 20–21, 22, 68, 69, 70–71, 72–73, 79 (middle), 90, 100–101, 112, 117, 118–119, 121, 122–123, 133 (top & middle), 150–151

Tekniska Museet, Stockholm 40–41

Ferdinand Urbahns, Eutin 79 (top), 120

U.S. National Archives 116, 138–139, 142–143, 144, 144–145, 146

U.S. Navy, Washington 6–7, 8–9, 16, 24–25, 26–27 (top), 54–55, 88, 88–89, 102–103, 118–119

Vickers Ltd 64–65 (bottom), 66–67 (bottom), 75 (bottom), 131, 157 (bottom)

1. THE WISHFUL ENTERPRISE

The summer of 1776 is memorable in more ways than one: in the dead of night not long after the signing of the Declaration of Independence a drama of some significance was being played out in New York harbour. A British patrol, keeping a watchful eye on His Majesty's warships anchored just off Staten Island, had spotted a strange-looking object moving slowly along the surface of the water. Rowing closer to investigate, the guard was brought up short by a deafening explosion. While this caused them no harm, the British were considerably shaken, and prudently decided to leave well enough alone. In any case, whatever it might be was moving away from the fleet and the unidentified but thoroughly sinister little engine of destruction was allowed to proceed on its course. The first submarine attack in the history of warfare had reached its unsuccessful conclusion.

This primitive warship, whimsically named *Turtle*, had been contrived by David Bushnell, an ex-Yale student in his mid-thirties. Bushnell had long been fascinated by the possibilities of underwater travel, but he had been galvanized into action the year before, when the long and acrimonious dispute between Britain and her mainland colonies had degenerated from words to war. An ardent patriot, Bushnell had from that moment devoted all his considerable energies to devising methods of clearing American waters of British ships. This enterprise, ambitious almost to the point of being fanciful, had more than a tinge of desperation about it. In a war with her colonies Britain's mastery of the seas was absolute, and it extended right to the harbours of her enemy. By the summer of 1776 the rebellious colonies were effectively blockaded. Washington's Continental Army was bottled up in New York City, and the newly signed Declaration of Independence rang more of defiance than of dedication.

So it was that George Washington paid keen attention to Bushnell's experiments, first with the matter of exploding gunpowder under water and then with the tricky business of floating mines—which were no more than weighted kegs of gunpowder—with the tides to his target. Frustrated by the vagaries of tidal movement, Bushnell turned from indirect to direct control of his new weapon. He built an admirably simple and workable one-man submarine. Made from wood after the manner of a barrel, the boat sat in the water like an upright egg, small end at the bottom. The name 'turtle' probably referred to her more or less resembling two giant turtle shells stuck together. Capped with a watertight hatch and ventilators that shut automatically on submerging, Bushnell's submarine belied its somewhat comical appearance, and the 150-pound keg of gunpowder nestled behind, just over the rudder, was anything but a joke. The principles of construction were sound: the *Turtle* had ample strength to resist pressure to the modest depths for which she

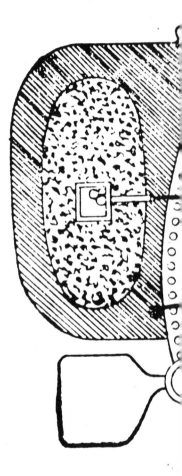

Right: A cutaway drawing of the *Turtle*. The ballast is controlled by foot, the two propellers and rudder by hand

8

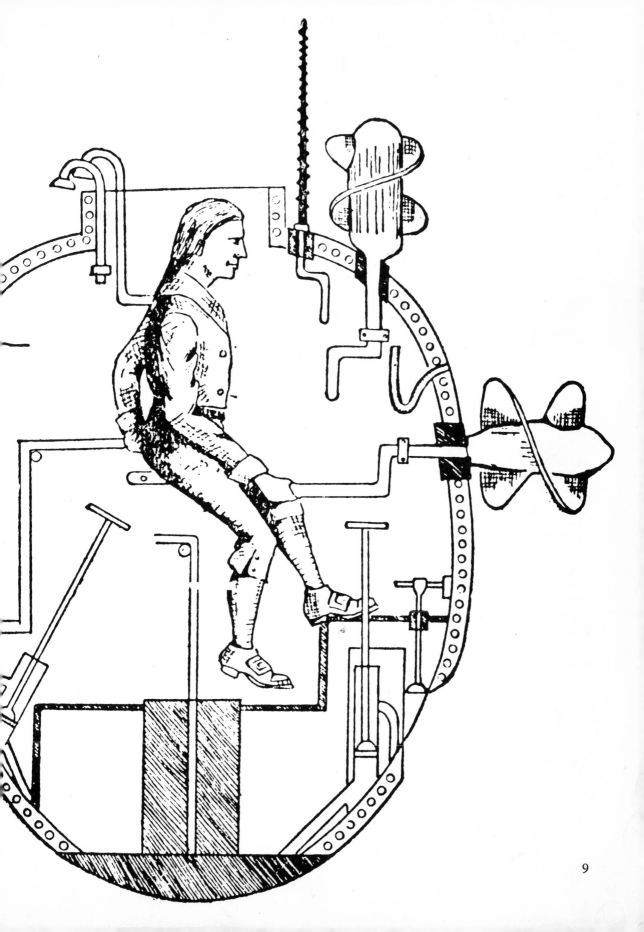

9

was intended, and, weighted with lead at the bottom to keep her upright, she demonstrated a great deal more stability underwater than would many later and more sophisticated efforts.

Within her limitations she possessed an equally practical method of locomotion. The operator looked through one of three small windows immediately below the hatch. With his foot he operated a pedal which opened a valve to admit water. When he was trimmed down almost flush with the waterline—never below it—he would proceed forward by cranking a handle which turned what was described as 'an oar, formed upon the principle of a screw'. In order to submerge, the operator worked a similar 'oar', or rudimentary propellor, positioned above the craft. This in effect dragged him under, and by carefully balancing the two controls (as well as the rudder) he could then move ahead. There was a water-gauge to indicate depth and a phosphorous-marked compass for reading the direction in the dark. The operator had enough air for thirty minutes under water, and when he wanted to rise he operated by hand two brass forcing pumps which ejected the water previously admitted. In an emergency he could jettison some of the lead ballast.

Positioned for attack, underneath an enemy ship, the intention was that the operator would screw an auger, which protruded above the *Turtle*, up into the planking. This auger was attached by a line to the keg of gunpowder, and once it was firmly screwed in the operator would then release both auger and keg. The keg, which was deliberately left buoyant, would float up to sit tight against the enemy's keel. A timing device would then set off the explosion after the submarine was out of harm's way. Altogether it was a cunningly devised and potentially lethal weapon, and it very nearly worked.

The target was H.M.S. *Eagle*, a 64-gun frigate standing, with supposed impunity, off New York. It was originally planned that Bushnell's brother, who was very familiar with the *Turtle*, would make the raid. When he became ill, however, the task fell to a volunteer, Sergeant Ezra Lee. Cloaked in darkness, and with the water as smooth as glass, the *Turtle* was towed out into the harbour by rowboats and cast adrift. Lee was on his own.

As instructed, he stayed just above the surface, with the hatch open and his head poked out the top, watching the tide carry him towards his destination. Unfortunately the tide had been misjudged and it swept him past the British warships; but he waited for it to slacken and then laboriously made his way towards the *Eagle*. When he was very close he shut the hatch, submerged, and manoeuvered into position directly beneath the frigate. Being this close he should have succeeded, but luck began to run against him. He found himself trying to screw the auger into a metal strap that was supporting the rudder hinge. Naturally it would not take, but with half an hour's air supply there should have been time for a second attempt elsewhere. But whether

Opposite: One of several mediaeval illustrations that show Alexander the Great being lowered into the depths

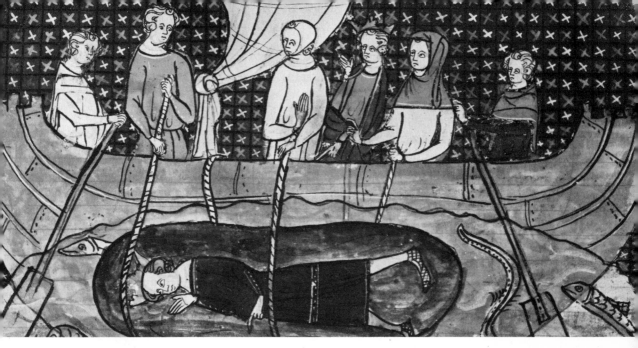

The title page of William
Bourne's *Inventions*, published
in 1578. The author explains
how a boat can be constructed
in such a way that it can be
submerged and surfaced at will

because of inexperience or because the tide was making it
awkward to remain stationary, Lee decided to abandon the
attack, surface, and head back to shore.

It was at this point that the British patrol stumbled upon him
and gave pursuit. The *Turtle* could not possibly outrun a row-
boat, and Lee had the presence of mind to release the mine and
activate the timing device. It is of some irony, therefore, that on
the first occasion a submarine launched a torpedo it did so in
self-defence. If she succeeded in that, Bushnell's *Turtle* also
succeeded at least partially towards the larger purpose. The
British hastily moved their warships further away from shore,
and determined to keep a closer look-out. For the rest, Bushnell
and his submarine had no further impact on the War of
Independence, although Washington later mentioned to
Jefferson that he considered it 'an effort of genius'. It was
undeniably that, but while Bushnell's was the first attempt to
use an underwater craft as a weapon of war it did not mark the
first appearance of a submarine boat.

The story of submarines begins well before the eighteenth
century, and indeed if one is a little loose with the definition of
'submarine' it begins over 2,000 years before. Alexander the
Great is reputed to have been lowered into the sea in a sort of
glass barrel, to have remained on the bottom for some time,
and then been raised again to the surface, whereupon he
delighted his listeners with wonderful descriptions of things
seen. This story is illustrated in several mediaeval manuscripts
(somewhat differently each time), and while it is probably
apocryphal, Alexander did have first-hand knowledge of underwater warfare. In 332 B.C. he was blockading the harbour at
Tyre when—and not for the first time in naval warfare—divers
cut the cables of his ships.

Ancient and mediaeval history are rife with examples of similar exploits by divers, and whether Alexander did or did not explore the depths the principle of the diving bell has been known for a very long time. A true submarine boat, however, is one that can be submerged and then *propelled* underwater, and the first recorded mention of such a vessel occurs in the writings of the Englishman William Bourne. In a book published in 1578 he gives a remarkably accurate, if painstaking exposition of the principles that govern the modern submarine. All that is necessary to make a boat that will go under the water and then surface at will, he explains, is to construct it in such a way that the volume of water it displaces can be varied. As he puts it, 'any magnitude of body that is in the water, if that the quantity of bignesse, having alwaies but one weight, may be made bigger or lesser, then it shall swimme when you would, and sinke when you list....' The way to vary the 'bignesse', he goes on, is to make 'the ioints or places that doo make the thing bigger or lesser ... of leather; and in the inside to have skrewes to winde it in and also out againe....' Bourne never put his theory to the test, but had he implemented his plans with the rigorous attention to detail that he shows in outlining them he would have stood an excellent chance of success.

It was not until forty-odd years later that a contrivance along the lines Bourne suggests made a recorded appearance. In 1620 Cornelis Drebbel, a Dutch physician who had long resided in England, began to delight Londoners with submarine displays. Unfortunately there are no contemporary drawings of any of his submarines (he built at least three) but references to Drebbel's spectacular demonstrations are too numerous and exact to allow much dispute over his title of 'the father of submarines'. Apparently the largest of the Drebbel submarines contained twelve rowers and still had enough room for an unspecified number of passengers, and it is claimed that King James I allowed himself to be conveyed in this manner the few miles from Westminster to Greenwich. This latter is extremely unlikely in view of the King's notorious physical cowardice, but it is true that he was an enthusiastic patron of Drebbel's—whose scientific and quasi-scientific interests embraced practically everything from explosives to perpetual motion. There is a maddening dearth of reliable information about these prototype submarines. There are cryptic references to a construction of greased leather over a wooden frame, an operational depth of 12 to 15 feet, goat-skin bags which could be filled with water for submerging and then be squeezed out for rising, Ben Jonson's comment about Drebbel's 'invisible eel' and, most frustrating of all, the staggering assertion that Drebbel could revitalize the air in his submarine by pouring out a few drops of some mysterious fluid that he carried in a bottle. Drebbel, it is said, believed that the greater portion of air was irrelevant to breathing and that what

Opposite 1: An eighteenth-century drawing of Drebbel's submarine. Twelve rowers provide the power, but it is not clear either from the drawing or contemporary reports how the submarine maintains stability underwater

2: Cornelis Drebbel, who built the first submarine on record in the early seventeenth century

3–4: The de Son submarine under construction and a cutaway drawing of the finished product. De Son made fantastic claims for his creation—all of them meaningless because the boat could not move

2

3

4

was important was 'a certain quintessence'. It was this quintessence that he kept in the bottle. Had he stumbled on the existence of oxygen? If so, what was the magical 'liquor' and what did he pour it on to release this element, unknown at the time? Either he died with the secret or else the information was not thought worth recording.

Oddly enough, the flurry of interest that surrounded Drebbel's experiments, and the visible proof that underwater navigation was possible, did not result in either a sudden or a steady progress along the path that he opened. Over the next 100 years there was considerable theorizing on the subject—some of it sound, much of it bizarre—but with a single exception it appears that no one tried to build an underwater boat. The exception is worth noting not for its performance but for its intent.

In 1653 a Frenchman named de Son laid down a vessel in Rotterdam which he confidently asserted was a warship of awesome menace. She was of impressive dimensions, 72 feet long, 12 feet high, and 8 feet wide. She would, boasted de Son, destroy 100 ships in a day, make the return journey to London in a day, the East Indies in six weeks, and withal 'run as swift as a bird can flye no fire, nor Storme, or Bullets, can hinder her . . .' Drawings of this ambitious craft survive, and indeed the iron-capped beam that runs her length and protrudes from both ends would have been an effective weapon against ships of the time— if, that is, the boat had been able to move. A 'wheele that goeth round' worked by some sort of clockwork contraption is not likely to power a 72-foot submarine, and has a whiff of gimcrackery about it.

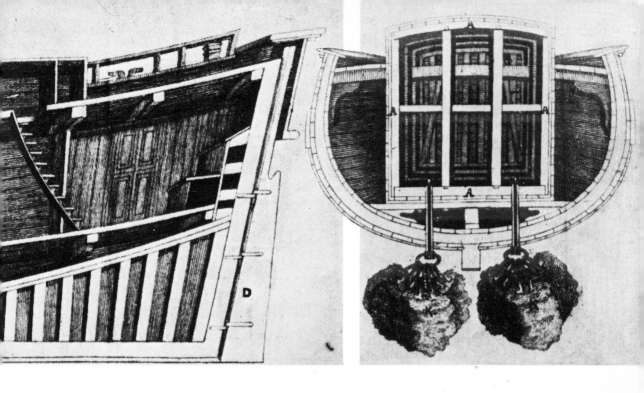

It was not until 1747 that another practicable underwater vessel appeared, again in England. Nathaniel Symons, a Devonshire carpenter, built and demonstrated a submarine not nearly so sophisticated as Drebbel's was supposed to have been, but one very much in keeping with Bourne's instructions. The boat was made up of two sections joined with leather, and from the inside Symons could control the water ballast by winding screws that drew the sections together accordion-fashion. This is perfectly feasible if the intention is simply to go down and up, and Symons does not appear to have concerned himself with propelling the submarine, although he may have been attacking the problem in stages. If so it is a pity that he was forced to give up for lack of funds, and he complained about this bitterly. Large crowds had turned up to watch him 'sink' into the River Dart, and many of the spectators were wealthy. Yet collections raised the derisory sum of a few shillings.

The idea of performing such underwater feats for money, as a form of entertainment or sport, crops up again in the 1770s. A Suffolk wheelwright named Day converted a Norwich market-boat by building a watertight cabin amidships and ballasting the thing until it sank. He claimed to have gone 30 feet to the bottom off Yarmouth and stayed there for twenty-four hours, rising to the surface again by detaching some of the ballast. Whether or not he exaggerated the endurance, Day managed to convince a wealthy gambler, Christopher Blake, that it was possible to remain submerged for much longer than a sceptical public would believe, and that herein lay a golden opportunity. Day announced that he would descend 100 feet for twelve hours, and his confederate began laying heavy wagers to that effect, on the understanding that Day should receive 10 per cent of the winnings. In June 1774 he went aboard a 50-ton sloop in Plymouth harbour, which he had converted along the same lines as his earlier boat: a roomy and watertight compartment and a great deal of ballast. His creature comforts included a hammock, a candle, a timepiece, biscuits, and water. Unhappily, what should be an amusing anecdote has a grim ending. There is a great difference between the water pressure at 30 feet and 100 feet, and neither Day nor his boat was ever seen again. At such a depth the wooden ship must simply have collapsed, and the wreckage been swept out to sea by the currents.

It should be evident from all this that there is no clear line of development running the century and a half from Drebbel to Bushnell, but rather episodic and on the whole futile attempts that neither improve on the former nor anticipate the latter. At the end of the eighteenth century, however, these two pioneers were joined by one of the most gifted inventors of all time.

Robert Fulton was an extraordinary man in so many ways that it is unfortunate to have to restrict ourselves to only one aspect of his career, and a secondary one at that. Born on a farm near Lancaster, Pennsylvania, in 1765, Fulton enjoyed little formal schooling—in his case perhaps an advantage. Although he had become an expert gunsmith while still in his teens, he made his opening mark in the world as a painter, and spent several years as a young man in England, working under the celebrated expatriate American Benjamin West. If only a competent painter, he was a highly talented draughtsman, and this latter skill was to stand him in good stead when he began to channel his energies in the direction that would bring him fame: as a civil and mechanical engineer.

These years in England, the late 1780s into the middle of the next decade, profoundly influenced Fulton's subsequent career in more ways than one. He began to turn increasingly from the easel to the drawing board, designing among other things an improved system for canal building. More important for our purposes, he found a cause, a rationale for developing what he fondly hoped would be the ultimate weapon. Like many of his contemporaries, Fulton had great sympathy with the ideals of the French Revolution, and despised a Britain that seemed bent on strangling liberty at birth as she had attempted twenty years earlier in Fulton's native America. Moreover he was of Irish descent, and had a keen awareness of the sufferings of that unhappy people at English hands. Either reason was sufficient to trigger hatred. Together they drove Fulton to implacable fury at Britain's overweaning influence in the world, and what he took to be its chief instrument, the Royal Navy. He determined to destroy it.

In 1796 Fulton therefore set to work designing a submarine

The American Robert Fulton, and a diagram of his submarine, *Nautilus,* showing how a torpedo (mine) could be attached to an enemy hull. Like other submarine pioneers Fulton held an inflated opinion of his crafts's potential. Under ideal conditions the *Nautilus* might well have accounted for an unlucky warship—but she was scarcely a threat to British navel supremacy

—KEY—

Body of Boat (Ellipsoid).
Metal Keel
Pumps
Metal Conning Tower.
Cross Bulkhead.
Propeller.
Vertical Rudder.
Horizontal Rudder.
Fulcrum for L
Gears for operation of L.
Horn of the "Nautilus".
Torpedo
The Bottom of a Vessel.

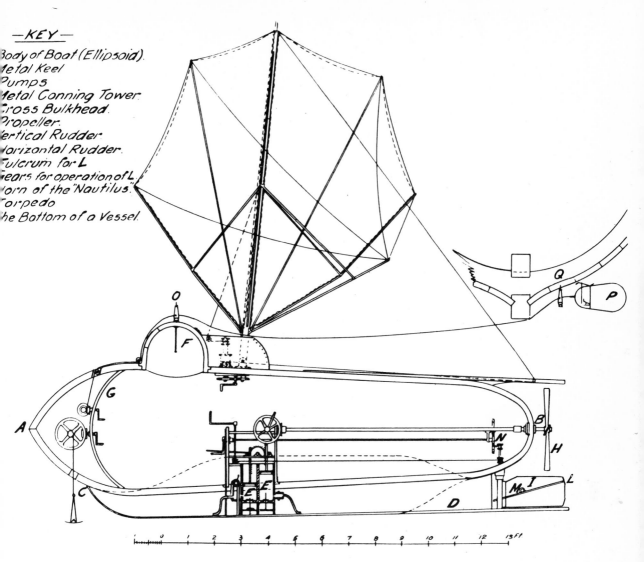

which, like Bushnell's, would be able stealthily to bring a lethal charge directly into contact with an enemy hull. The following year he took his plans to France and presented them to the Directory with the bland assertion that he was bringing them the means to ruin their traditional enemy. He would 'annihilate their Navy', but for a price: money for each ship destroyed, prize rights, and regular commissions for himself and all crew members. This latter point was crucial, and it was over it that negotiations broke down. Fulton was convinced, probably rightly, that submarine warfare would be bracketed with the use of fireships as an atrocity, and that to be taken in action would mean summary execution as a war criminal. But if the submarine crews were commissioned, and if the French were to let it be known that the very bloodiest reprisals would be taken against English prisoners of war should harm befall them, then he was perfectly willing to accept the normal risks of battle. The Minister of Marine was not unhappy at the prospect of British

17

Left: Fulton's *Nautilus* underway. The novel addition of a
sail and collapsible mast was
meant to ensure speedy progress
on the surface

warships going to the bottom, by fair means or foul, but it was
quite another matter to announce to the world that it was official
French policy to ignore the rules of war. Fulton's proposals were
turned down.

With characteristic persistence, Fulton refused to take no for
an answer. He put together a model of his submarine (already
named *Nautilus*), and turned up the next year to put the same
proposal to a new Minister of Marine. This time he received a
more sympathetic hearing, and a commission was set up to
examine the *Nautilus*. It reported favourably—choosing to
ignore the ethical questions—but the Directory again refused to
proceed. In view of this 'irrational' decision Fulton despaired of
the French and moved to Holland, where he encountered a
similar lack of enthusiasm. It looked very much as though the
Nautilus would never see the light of day, and the British fleet
would continue to roam with its customary insolence. The
breakthrough came with Napoleon's rise to power, and the

consequent arrival of yet another Minister of Marine, this time one who was an enthusiast. Authorization was granted, and the *Nautilus* was finally built.

By this point Fulton had had plenty of time to think out his design, and what finally emerged was an ingenious little craft. The *Nautilus* was 21 feet long and bullet-shaped; she was copper-built over an iron frame, and included a collapsible mast and sail to allow easy surface mobility. She was surmounted with a dome-like conning tower with glass scuttles. The system of controlling water ballast was similar to Bushnell's, and underwater propulsion came from a hand-driven propellor.

In the summer of 1800 Fulton began his trials, and while initially he found it difficult to control both depth and direction he gradually became more skilful. Naturally he was extremely eager to test his secret weapon under combat conditions and, armed with a detachable mine, again similar in concept to Bushnell's, he transported the *Nautilus* to Brest, from where he determined to launch his strikes. These came to nothing—he could never manage to get close enough to his quarry—and a cynic would argue that it was these disappointing results which brought the morality of his enterprise under renewed scrutiny. Again the Ministry of Marine changed hands, and with icy disdain Fulton was told that his device was 'fit only for Algerians and pirates'. Even more damning, Napoleon had, quite independent of all side issues, come to the conclusion that the American was little more than a glib confidence-trickster, an adventurer motivated by the love of money not the love of France.

It was a harsh judgment but it does gain some credence from Fulton's next move. He slipped across the channel under an assumed name and took his invention to the British Prime Minister, William Pitt. Pitt jumped at it, and promptly set up a high-powered commission to investigate both the submarine and the quite independent notion of underwater mines, or 'torpedoes' as all such devices were then known. The commission reported that the underwater boat was a chimera but that mines could be a deadly threat to shipping. To prove the latter point, Fulton was allowed to attach a mine to the 200-ton Danish brig, *Dorothea*, and he later recorded with gleeful satisfaction how one of the officials present had pompously asserted that 'if a torpedo were placed under his cabin while he was at dinner, he would feel no concern for the consequences'. Twenty minutes later the *Dorothea* was literally blasted out of the water. Fulton was not slow to point out that such mines were a heaven-sent defence against a threatened French invasion, and that his expertise was therefore worth a great deal of money.

For a time it seemed as though the Admiralty would seriously implement the scheme, and Fulton was encouraged by the offer

Below: The *Dorothea* is blown to bits by a Fulton torpedo. It was a startling demonstration of the destructive power of an underwater explosion

of £100,000 to lend his talents exclusively to that navy whose destruction had long been his passion. But his Nemesis struck again: a reshuffle in the Admiralty and the death of Pitt left him at the mercy of his enemies. And chief amongst these was the First Lord of the Admiralty, Earl St Vincent. After listening to Fulton describe the *Dorothea* experiment, St Vincent replied with the brusque dismissal that would become enshrined as naval dogma for nearly a hundred years: 'Pitt was the greatest fool that ever existed, to encourage a mode of war which they who commanded the seas did not want, and which, if successful, would deprive them of it.' If there was any doubt about how sea battles should be fought, Nelson had just resolved them at Trafalgar.

This final blow drove the inventor back to his native America, without money and with no reputation preceding him. Ten years of unremitting effort had got him nowhere, and a lesser man might have lowered his sights and been content with a decent obscurity. Yet defeat was really a blessing in disguise, for in the absence of the sort of motor power that would not be available for many years to come, there was no prospect of building a submarine with a useful performance. Fulton was better off leaving it alone, and bringing his fertile imagination to bear on that quite different project which was to bring him dramatic

Earl St Vincent, implacably hostile to Fulton's weapon and scathing in his denunciation of the Prime Minister, William Pitt, for having lent support to it

success: the application of steam power to surface craft.

A less gifted engineer but no less fascinating character came to submarine warfare at mid century. The German states were at war with Denmark, and the Germans had no navy with which to counter the Danish blockade of her North Sea ports. William Bauer, an artillery corporal, came forward with a submarine design and argued his case with enough eloquence to get official backing. The submarine *Brandtaucher* was in the Bushnell-Fulton mould, and came no closer to achieving her designer's goal, although her presence did force the Danish ships to stand off further. Unlike his predecessors, Bauer came within an inch of getting killed by his creation. On one of the trials he submerged in Kiel harbour with two crewmen. The *Brandtaucher* went out of control and plunged nose first to the bottom and stuck fast, with water pouring in through parts of the hull that had collapsed under pressure. With great coolness, Bauer persuaded his crew—who thought him deranged—to sit tight and assist the entry of yet more water, until the pressure of the air trapped in the submarine equalled the water pressure outside. They then could—and did—open the hatch at the rear and escape. He was right, of course, but it is not easy to gamble one's life on abstract theory.

German interest did not survive the loss of Bauer's prototype,

An early twentieth-century model of William Bauer's *Brandtaucher*. Like his predecessors, Bauer discovered that his submarine was more menacing in theory than in practice

Left: The interior of the
Brandtaucher. A pair of treadmills provide the power

Above: An illustration of the
charming incident supposed to
have taken place in Kronstadt
harbour. An orchestra aboard
the *Diable Marin* plays the
Russian national anthem to
mark the coronation of Tsar
Alexander II

and he was forced to begin the pilgrimage that Fulton knew so
well. He managed to arouse interest in both Austria and England
but nothing more; in Russia, on the other hand, he got funds
to build another submarine. The *Diable Marin* was a more
ambitious craft than her predecessor: 52 feet long and over
12 feet wide. She still relied on muscle-power (treadmills), which
was unavoidable, but Bauer's method of attaching the mine to
its target was unnecessarily primitive. A 500-pound explosive
was to be carefully positioned manually by an operator working
inside long rubber gloves that protruded from the craft. The
Diable Marin did not live up to her name and never saw military
action, although Bauer did manage to demonstrate her success-
fully, and on one occasion with startling effect. The story does
not have the ring of incontrovertible truth, but apparently to
mark the coronation of Tsar Alexander II on 6 September
1856, Bauer submerged in Kronstadt harbour. He carried a
skeleton orchestra with him and, shortly after, strains of the
Russian national anthem wafted across the water.

It will be apparent that so far the submarine, or submersible
boat, had demonstrably failed to measure up to any of the claims
made for it. It had neither assisted in underwater exploration
nor become the scourge of surface warships. Whatever its
potential (and as a mine-layer even the most primitive submarine
had potential) it had proved hazardous only to its crews, and in
large measure it could be written off as the plaything of
eccentrics. Little more than a hundred years ago it must have
seemed as though St Vincent had been unduly concerned.

23

2. A GLIMMER OF SUCCESS

Leaving aside Fulton's theatrical challenge to the entire British navy, the tactical use of the submarine, such as it was, had so far been limited to attempts at blockade-raising. Enthusiasts saw the invisible gunboat as the one—and only—way in which a weaker naval power could drive a stronger fleet away from its shores. Admittedly neither Bushnell nor Bauer had managed to damage, much less sink, a vessel but they had shown how the very *fear* of their presence could drive surface warships into a defensive posture. The American Civil War of 1861–5 provided yet another challenge to a weaker combatant to devise means of thwarting a blockade. Despite early and spectacular successes on the ground, by the second year of the war the Confederacy faced a crippling and potentially decisive blockade; imaginative strategists again turned their attention to underwater warfare. Whereas previous submarine 'campaigns' were merely individual attempts with somewhat sceptical official support, the Civil War marks a serious attempt by a belligerent to tip the scales with a new weapon. The attempt failed but it did prove much, not least the stark fact that an armed submarine could destroy a surface warship.

While it is not known exactly how many Confederate submarines were built, by all earlier standards they were mass produced: no less than nine fell into Union hands when they captured Charleston and its harbour. One reason why the total can only be guessed is that the submarines were not given individual names, but were collectively known as 'Davids'—an optimistic reference to their giant-killing promise. As well as marking a new departure in naval policy the Davids embodied some striking innovations. In the first place they were scarcely submarines at all. They were small steam-powered ironclads, ballasted to run awash with so little superstructure showing above the surface as to present a negligible target, at least by night. They were equipped with a spar torpedo in the form of a potent charge stuck well out in front on the end of a beam— with luck far enough out to prevent suicide. The spar torpedo sounds dangerous to all concerned, and so it was to prove.

In fact the David, whether or not it should properly be called a submarine, has a strong claim to being the most hazardous warship ever conceived, and if the crews did not require the fanaticism of *kamikaze* pilots they certainly needed the blind courage. The fault with the David was basic, and could have been foreseen. It was obvious that steam would provide a vastly improved performance over manpower, but that meant having an open hatch to get air for the boiler. It is inviting disaster to hurtle along with the bulk of a ship under water and an open hatch just above the surface. Indeed the danger is so real and present that it is difficult to understand why it was even attempted once, let alone adopted as a standard method of operation. What happens if a ship passes by and sends out waves that break over

Previous pages: A Confederate David aground in Charleston harbour at the end of the American Civil War

Below: Sketch of the night attack on U.S.S. *Ironsides* by a David, October 1863

Above: Drawing of C.S.S. *Hunley*, the first submarine to sink a warship (February 1864). A total of thirty-five crew members perished aboard the *Hunley* in five separate disasters

the hatch? This occurred at least once, and of course the David was swamped, as it would as easily have been by heavy seas, or a slight plunge. Once swamped the David would sink immediately giving the crew members almost no chance of escape; short of a miracle they must either drown or suffocate. Having said this it remains true that the David was well enough designed for its purpose of attacking blockading ships.

Soon after darkness had fallen on the night of 5 October 1863 a great explosion shook the Union warship *Ironsides*, a heavily-armed ironclad which formed part of the blockade outside Charleston. Moments before the watch had reported something resembling a log approaching, but there was no time to take evasive or any kind of defensive action. Either the spar torpedo exploded just before contact was made or it did so on and not below the waterline, but in any case the *Ironsides* was only slightly damaged. In the aftermath of the explosion the David was swamped, although its commander, Lieutenant Glassell, and two crew members had the presence of mind to abandon ship just before this happened. According to one report Glassell was captured but the other two swam back to the David, which was miraculously still afloat. They clambered aboard, relit the fires (which had been doused), and made good their escape.

The following year a different kind of submarine appeared. Sometimes referred to as a David but more often as a *Hunley* after her designer, this new submarine differed from her predecessors in two important respects. Shaped like a long, very thin cigar, she was hand-powered by eight men staggered along a crankshaft that ran most of the 60-foot length. Because there

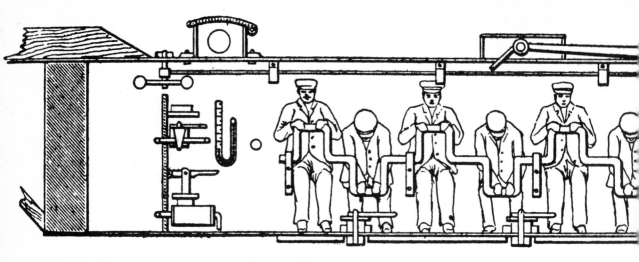

was no need for an air supply (at least as long as there was enough for the men to breathe), the *Hunley* was designed to run completely submerged for the short distance needed to complete a surprise attack. The transition from awash to submerged was accomplished by means of a pair of rudders positioned horizontally.

The *Hunley*'s great weakness lay in her disproportionate length, which made the craft even more difficult to control when awash (or submerged for that matter) than the earlier Davids. It was given to plunging steeply with the slightest provocation, and while this is a hazardous failing in a submerged boat which has tightly shut hatches, it is, as has been explained, quite lethal in an awash boat which is running with hatches open. Yet successive crews persisted in operating the *Hunley* in just such a manner. Doubtless they were motivated by the wish for a constant supply of fresh air, but it also seems likely that they suffered from the delusion of feeling safer with the sky above them rather than the waves. If one imagines being jammed into a long, narrow, and dark tube, and given the choice of going under the water or staying around the surface with a 'door' open, it is easy to see the fatal attraction. And fatal it was. During trials the *Hunley* sank four times, twice killing most aboard, twice claiming all. These are chilling statistics and it seems inconceivable that sane men would have persevered. Yet the *Hunley* was raised again, fitted out with another crew, and sent directly into action without further trials.

Under the command of an infantry lieutenant by the name of Dixon, the *Hunley* crept out of Charleston harbour on the evening of 17 February 1864. Around nine o'clock the submarine was seen bearing down on the new Union sloop-of-war *Housatonic*, but again too late for anything to be done about it. The spar torpedo struck home and a mighty explosion tore the *Housatonic*'s side wide open. She sank quickly, in shallow water, but while there was only time for one lifeboat to make off the

Interior of the *Hunley*, showing how the eight crewmen provide power. In this drawing the hatches are closed but in practice they were left open— with catastrophic results. The submarine was sixty feet long, and the cross-section (right) shows how narrow she was in proportion. This made for great instability

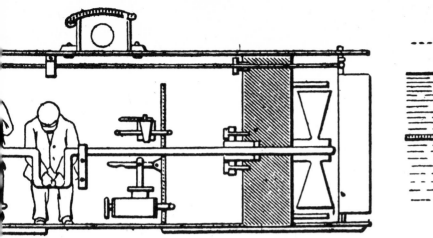

casualties were light. Immediately after the explosion the *Hunley* vanished, and it was first thought that she had escaped during the confusion. Several years later, after the war, divers investigating the wreckage of the *Housatonic* found the submarine lying close alongside. What had happened was that the water which rushed into the side of the stricken *Housatonic* had sucked the bow of the *Hunley* in with it. Thus trapped by her victim she had been carried to the bottom. The loss of a complete fifth crew brought the *Hunley*'s grim total to thirty-five, and it marked the end of submarine activity during the war.

Despite her harvest of death the *Hunley* has some claim to recognition as the first successful submarine, in the limited sense of having managed to destroy a surface vessel. Yet in other respects she showed no advance on much earlier efforts, being hand-powered, difficult to control, and unsafe to a degree that would have made Bushnell and Fulton recoil in horror. By coincidence, while the *Hunley* and other Davids were floundering about Charleston Harbour, in another part of the world the wraps were coming off a submarine of astonishing sophistication.

The principal reason why submarine technology made so little progress between Drebbel and Hunley is that there was no improvement at all in the crucial matter of motive power: after two-and-a half centuries human muscle-power was still the only driving force. True, in the intervening years steam had revolutionized any number of industrial processes and had made a dramatic impact on transportation. Yet while steam power was so obviously well suited to movement by rail and by surface ship it was not the answer for submarines—or for aeroplanes, airships, and horseless carriages, to pick obvious examples. Real and lasting progress in all these areas would have to await the development of a suitable engine, and that development was still some years away. Towards the end of the 1850s the French Minister of Marine thought the solution was at hand. He passed over to a shipbuilder plans that had been drawn up some

years earlier for a revolutionary submarine. More than that he commissioned such a craft for the navy, and by 1863 *Le Plongeur* was ready to be launched.

She was a remarkable sight, 140 feet long and with a displacement of 420 tons—by far the largest submarine to appear before the twentieth century. The reason for the great size was that the 80-horsepower engine ran on compressed air, and vast quantities of it. Much of *Le Plongeur* was no more than storage space for enormous bottles of 'fuel'. Eighty horsepower is not much for a craft of such a size, but the main problem centered on underwater stability. The ability to keep a depth line would long plague submarine designers and crew, but *Le Plongeur* was particularly erratic in this respect, mainly because she was very long and flat. What happened during trials was that on the surface she behaved well enough, and settled into the awash position unprotestingly after the correct amount of ballast had been added. But when, in order to submerge completely, the final ballast was admitted so as to reduce buoyancy to nothing, 'zero buoyancy' as it is called, she surged out of control. Neither horizontal rudders nor an ingenious compressed air device calculated to adjust weight could rectify this. *Le Plongeur* followed much the pattern of a playful dolphin, but for the crew it was in deadly earnest. She would plummet downwards at a steep angle, and all the correcting gear would immediately swing into action. After a momentary delay she would make a break for

Above: The French submarine *Le Plongeur* being towed out to sea for trials. She was an extraordinarily advanced design for the 1860s—very large and powered by an 80-horsepower compressed air engine

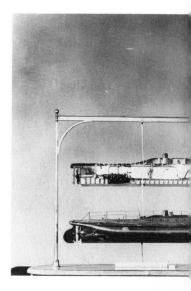

the surface, where another 'correction' would start the process all over again. For all the technical advances she embodied, *Le Plongeur* was a failure, and while the French navy had the sense to realize this they did not have the enterprise to build on what was a very real foundation. They abandoned the idea altogether.

The story now becomes somewhat confusing, for two reasons. During the closing decades of the century the field became crowded, as a rapidly growing number of individuals and governments grasped the central truth that the working submarine was just over the horizon. This surge of interest, especially in the 1880s, resulted in much overlapping and duplication, so that it is difficult in many cases to see who is setting the pace and whether he is doing so by independent and original genius or by skilful adaptation. Secondly, the final breakthrough in such a complex engineering feat as the modern submarine is usually not as climactic as a dramatist would wish. The process can be likened to several artists working on a large mural, not as a team but each determined to claim the mural as his own and above all to provide the finishing touches. An observer would find it difficult to say at what point and with what daub of paint the surface was transformed from almost-mural to mural.

It would be impossible here to discuss the work of everyone who contributed in some measure to the modern submarine. Nevertheless a few individuals stand out clearly, most clearly of all the Irish-American John Holland. Holland's obsession with underwater warfare stemmed from exactly the same source as did Fulton. He loathed England and (like Fulton), he focused his hatred on the Royal Navy. The submarine would be the great equalizer. Holland arrived in the United States in 1873 and took up a teaching post in Paterson, New Jersey. Apparently he had given considerable thought to submarine boats before leaving Ireland, but nothing came of this interest until a timely misfortune struck him in his adopted land. Out walking on a winter's day he slipped and fell on an icy patch, breaking his leg. Several months of enforced idleness followed—during which Holland progressed from thinking about submarines to actually sketching out detailed plans for one.

In 1875 he was persuaded by friends to send in these plans to the Secretary of the Navy; they were rejected out of hand, on the grounds that no one would willingly go down in such a craft, that in any case a submarine could not be navigated when submerged, and finally—much more to the point—Washington was little inclined to indulge flights of fancy. This latter was certainly true but it had not always been the case, at least with regard to submarines. Three years before, the government had actually paid out $50,000 for a small hand-operated submarine known as the *Intelligent Whale*. She had proved a total failure and it was doubtless her embarrassing memory that prompted

Below: Scale models of *Le Plongeur*, the top one showing the interior layout. As with all pioneer submarines the overriding difficulty was in keeping a steady depth line—exacerbated in this case by the great length (160 feet)

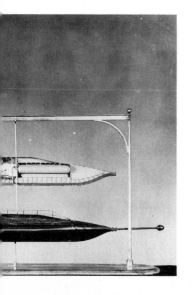

the cursory dismissal of Holland's scheme. Private backing would therefore have to be found, and this proved surprisingly easy.

There was active in the United States at this time an organization which not only shared Holland's Anglophobia but existed for the sole purpose of fomenting revolution in Ireland: the Fenian Society. Founded in 1858, the society reached its zenith in the years following the Civil War, and while an optimistic invasion of Canada in 1866 miscarried—and embarrassed the U.S. government—the dream of humbling mighty England lived on. The tactics advocated would not be out of place in a handbook for modern revolutionaries: hit-and-run terrorism aimed at sapping the morale of an enemy too powerful to confront openly. It is easy to see why the submerged gunboat would appeal. After witnessing a splendid demonstration with a 30-inch clockwork model, Fenian leaders cheerfully placed $6,000 from their 'skirmishing fund' at the inventor's disposal. For their money they got *Holland I,* a one-man submarine that has been preserved and to the modern eye looks as though it might have been put together from a giant meccano set. The 14-foot craft was little more than a diving boat, and had Holland stopped there he would scarcely rate a footnote in submarine history. When she was launched in July 1878—fortunately unmanned—*Holland I* promptly sank because, as it was discovered later, two small screw-plugs were missing from the bottom. She was hauled up, pumped dry, and refloated, this time with Holland at the controls. While the primitive combustion engine did not work at all, the submarine duly sank and rose at Holland's command, and in the course of lengthy trials he learned a great deal to augment his theoretical knowledge. It is this, in fact, that stamps Holland as a great inventor. His first submarine was little advance on many that had appeared earlier—and in no way comparable to the ambitious *Le Plongeur*—but he never saw it as any more than a prototype. When he had learned all he could he carefully stripped *Holland I* of anything that could be of further use and scuttled the shell. He set about building another submarine, again with Fenian money, and this one was of a different order entirely.

The Fenians were satisfied with *Holland I* as far as it went, and the delights of conspiracy had been heightened by the suspicion that British spies were lurking at the trials. But they wanted a warship, and *Holland I* was certainly not that. Deftly skirting all the practical difficulties, they had concocted a grandiose scheme for settling old scores, and settling them with a vengeance. They had originally seized on the submarine idea as an ingenious method of harassing British ships that were unlucky enough to come within range—within range of what was not at all clear but it was blithely assumed that some suitably lethal weapon would turn up. But it was clear to all that such a sporadic war of

The American John Holland emerges from the conning tower of the submarine that bears his name. Entering the field in the 1870s, Holland persevered through chronic misfortunes, and, by the turn of the century, he stood at the forefront of submarine development

attrition would be a very long and drawn-out affair. There were any number of British ships and no matter how methodically they were whittled away the world's largest shipbuilding industry was probably capable of making good the losses. Why not go to the heart of the matter and obliterate the Royal Navy? Was this not the one sure way to bring England to her knees? It was soberly resolved therefore to have Holland build a number of well-armed submarines, large enough to operate effectively under combat conditions but small enough so that they could be tucked into the hold of a merchant ship; a specially constructed watertight hold that would be below the waterline and flooded so that the submarines could be unobtrusively floated in. The ship would then cross the Atlantic and proceed in supposed innocence from harbour to harbour looking for the fleet or at least a substantial portion of it. Having stalked the enemy to its lair—where it would doubtless be off guard—the mother ship would release her submarines, whose underwater guns would be unanswerable. After spending their ammunition the submarines would scuttle back to safety, and in the wild confusion that would ensue the merchantman would slip away.

What Holland thought of this mad scheme is not known, but in 1881 he completed the submarine which was fondly expected to accomplish all the mischief: *Holland II*, the legendary *Fenian Ram*. She was a dramatic advance on *Holland I*, and in many respects the most advanced submarine to date. Still fairly small, 31 feet long and displacing 19 tons, *Holland II* had one of the earliest internal combustion engines, a Brayton, developing 15 horsepower. This engine worked imperfectly, but Holland

Above: Holland's *Fenian Ram* on view in Paterson, New Jersey. Built in 1881 and powered by an early gasoline engine, the *Fenian Ram* was the triumph of Holland's early career. But his financial backers, the Fenians, found to their annoyance that the inventor seemed more interested in running exhaustive trials than in attacking British ships

Right: A Whitehead torpedo knifes through the water after being fired from above the surface. It was this potent new weapon that would make the submarine a devastatingly effective warship

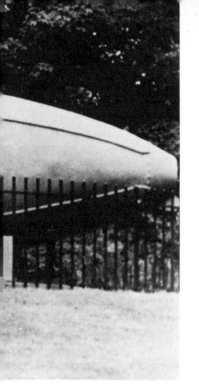

was on the right track. Moreover he showed great ingenuity in his approach to the problem of longitudinal stability, the bugbear of all submarine pioneers. As Holland saw it, most of their troubles stemmed from the mistaken belief that a submarine should—or must—be ballasted to zero buoyancy in order to submerge. Consequently the *Fenian Ram* always maintained a small reserve of positive buoyancy and was submerged not by 'sinking' but by 'diving'. This was accomplished by means of horizontal rudders, fitted at the stern along with the normal vertical rudder. Under power and with the diving rudders set down aft the boat would tip forward and force her way under the water. When the desired depth was reached the rudders would be reset at the angle required to establish and maintain equilibrium between the downward forces set up by the rudder action and the upward force of the reserve buoyancy. In theory this is ideally simple and straightforward but it required a very nice touch at the controls, which Holland certainly possessed.

The *Fenian Ram* became a familiar sight in the lower reaches of the Hudson River over the next two years as Holland put her through seemingly endless trials, modifying her slightly here and

there but above all gaining priceless experience in handling the craft. His backers were delighted with the results, but was it not time to start thinking about gaining some experience in the important matter of sinking British ships? Holland continued with the trials. And in any case, while the *Fenian Ram* was armed, she had not the firepower to take on a trawler let alone a battle-ship. She was fitted with a pneumatic cannon, 11 feet long and with a 9-inch bore, which would fire a 6-foot torpedo under-water. The gun worked, in the sense that it ejected the missile at speed. The trouble was, the torpedo had an unsettling habit of carrying along in a straight line for only a few feet before making a break for the surface and actually shooting high into the air. Holland himself recounted how, on one of the very few occasions the gun was actually fired, the unarmed torpedo hurtled out of the water to crash close by a fisherman, who was dozing in what he thought was perfect safety away from and well above the water. It seemed that the underwater gunboat had finally arrived but without the underwater gun. In fact, the two had arrived at almost the same time, and their marriage can be taken as the single most important development in submarine history.

Several years before Holland began his experiments, the English manager of an engineering firm at Fiume, Robert Whitehead, was approached by an Austrian naval captain who wanted his advice. Captain Luppis had a design for what he called a locomotive torpedo, that is a torpedo that was not just a large 'bullet' but was self-propelled. His inventive powers had failed him when it came to designing a practical method of propelling and more important guiding the torpedo, and his original idea was faintly ludicrous: the torpedo, really a miniature boat stuffed with explosives, was powered by either steam or clockwork, and was kept to its course by guide-ropes running out from shore. It was not much to go on but Whitehead accepted the challenge, and within two years he developed a working model that immediately rendered all other torpedoes obsolete. Only 14 inches in diameter, and carrying an 18-pound charge, the first Whitehead torpedo ran on compressed air for a couple of hundred yards at a speed of 6 knots, at a somewhat unsteady depth but in a reasonably straight line. The British Admiralty promptly dispatched observers to witness this phenomenon, and as a result of their report Whitehead was invited to England in 1870 with his latest models. These were a startling improvement on the original. They carried nearly four times the charge a thousand yards at a higher speed. Show-ing unsuspected far-sightedness, the Admiralty encouraged Whitehead to pursue his experiments, and in 1872 he opened a torpedo factory. There was steady progress in range, explosive power, and depth-keeping, and with the addition of a gyroscope mechanism the Whitehead torpedo became extraordinarily accurate. The gyroscope maintains its direction when it is spinning rapidly, and does this regardless of external forces. The 'Obry gear' (named after the inventor Ludwig Obry) uses this property to keep the torpedo running in a straight line: the gyroscope, sensitive to the slightest movement to left or right, instantly corrects the drift by acting upon the steering rudder. With this innovation the Whitehead torpedo became a weapon of terrible menace, in effect an explosive miniature submarine which was a great deal swifter and more predictable in its movements than any existing submarine. It was a far cry from a keg of gunpowder or a charge of dynamite stuck on the end of a spar.

By a curious oversight, what seems to modern eyes a most obvious connection between torpedo and submarine was not immediately spotted. The Whitehead torpedo was snapped up by the world's navies but for use in fast surface craft, and this touched off a tremendous vogue for torpedo-boats. It was surely inevitable, however, that the logic of firing the invisible weapon from the invisible boat would soon become apparent. The chain of events that finally linked the two underwater devices began with an unwarlike English clergyman, the Reverend George Garrett.

Garrett was, in fact, one of the few submarine enthusiasts who was not primarily concerned with sea power. In 1878 he launched a small hand-powered craft, and followed this up the next year with a much larger and more advanced submarine, the *Resurgam*. Forty-five feet long and cylindrical with sharply tapered ends, the *Resurgam* was intended by her designer to open up the fascinating world of underseas exploration. For whatever purpose, this submarine was a development of significance. In the first place the *Resurgam* was steam-powered underwater as well as on the surface. This was not as unfeasible as it may sound: with the firstes shut down and the funnel sealed off the massive boiler retained sufficient heat to drive the engine for a considerable time—and the submarine for several miles. At the same time Garrett arrived at Holland's conclusion about positive buoyancy, only he employed forward rather than aft diving rudders or hydroplanes. It is not, however, for these novel features that the *Resurgam* is most important; rather it is for the interest she aroused in another quarter. Her own career ended tragically when she was lost with a crew of three during trials, but by the time this had happened Garrett and his submarine had come to the attention of Thorsten Nordenfelt, the Swedish industrialist already famous for the quick-firing Nordenfelt gun.

The proliferation of torpedo-boats had sparked a corresponding obsession with torpedo-boat destroyers, high-speed craft capable of dealing with a torpedo-boat before the latter could bring its deadly weapon to bear. Nordenfelt, having invented the weapon which in his opinion dismissed the torpedo-boat as a serious threat, began looking for another method of employing

Garrett's *Resurgam*, photographed in 1879, a year
after she was built. She employed
steam power both on the
surface and when submerged

the Whitehead torpedo. If the quick-firing gun made it suicidal for a surface craft to bring the Whitehead within range, was not the answer to conceal the torpedo-boat underwater? In turning to submarines, therefore, Nordenfelt was seeking a counter to his own weapon.

In collaboration with Garrett, Nordenfelt began construction on his first submarine in 1881. The Swede had sufficient confidence (and money) to skip the usual first stage of a tiny prototype, and *Nordenfelt I* emerged as a large and technically advanced submarine. Sixty-four feet long, with a 9-foot beam,

Nordenfelt I under construction in Sweden 1882. Three years later she was launched in a blaze of publicity

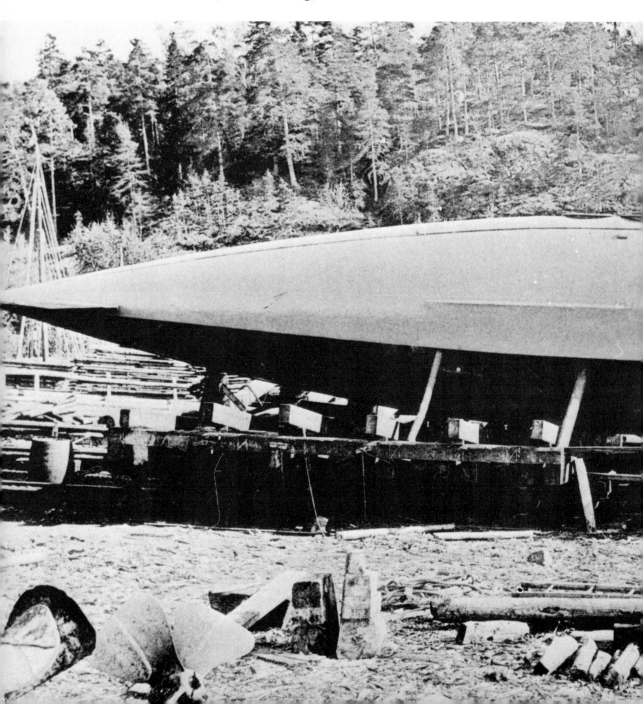

and 60 tons displacement, she was, like the *Resurgam*, steam-powered. But because Nordenfelt was adamant about the need always to keep absolutely level, as well as to retain positive buoyancy, his submarine employed a novel method of submerging. She was in effect hauled under the water by horizontal propellers fitted either side. Once under, this longitudinal stability was maintained by forward and aft hydroplanes. A Whitehead torpedo was carried in a tube fitted in the bow.

Because Nordenfelt, alone among those engaged in submarine work, brought reputation to the task as well as ability, his

submarine attracted a great deal of attention. *Nordenfelt I* began trials in the autumn of 1885 off Landskrona, Sweden, and not only naval experts but a galaxy of European royalty turned up to watch, including the Prince of Wales, the King and Queen of Denmark, and the Empress of Russia. Practically every nation in the world with pretence to naval power was represented, and if the trials were inconclusive they certainly touched off a flurry of interest. *Nordenfelt I* was purchased by the Greek government.

The major weakness in the Nordenfelt design was that it attempted to provide two things at once. Powered by steam, armed with the Whitehead torpedo, and operated awash with plenty of positive buoyancy, the Nordenfelt submarine was virtually a torpedo-boat. But it was inferior to a genuine torpedo-boat because it sacrificed speed and stability in order to fulfil its function as a submarine. Here again the compromise was a hindrance. While steam was ideal for surface power it had at least two serious disadvantages underwater. As can be readily imagined, when the hatches were shut down the great quantity of boiling hot water stored in the boiler and the reserve tanks quickly raised the temperature within the submarine, reportedly to an unbearable degree. Secondly, once submerged—and it was an unnecessarily laborious method of submerging—*Nordenfelt I* rivalled *Le Plongeur* for longitudinal instability; this despite her designer's iron rule that complete stability at all times was vital. Given the type of submarine he built Nordenfelt had reason to fear instability. Unlike ballast tanks, the boiler was never either completely full or completely

Nordenfelt I underway. She was purchased by Greece but proved of little naval value— and indeed was only operated on the surface

empty, so the slightest inclination would cause all this 'loose' water to shift in the direction of the tilt and thereby increase it. Despite all precautions this is precisely what did happen and it was a chronic failing in all Nordenfelt submarines.

The Greeks were prudent enough never to use *Nordenfelt I* submerged. A second *Nordenfelt*, much larger than her predecessor, was bought by Turkey but proved if anything even more difficult to control submerged. A third ran aground while being delivered to Russia and was scrapped.

By this time, the late 1880s, a host of inventors had entered the lists, and official interest was not limited to the governments of Greece, Turkey, and Russia. In 1886 the French Minister of Marine, Admiral Aube, overruled his advisors and ordered two submarines from separate sources. Ten years earlier a Russian engineer named Drzwiecki had engaged in submarine construction with little success, but he did employ an imaginative device for controlling both horizontal and vertical direction: a propellor fixed to a universal joint. This universal joint had been devised by the Frenchman Goubet, and it was to Goubet that the Admiral now turned. *Goubet I* appeared the following year, a little two-man craft that performed well enough within the limits imposed by her size and power. But Goubet did not consider her merely as a scaled down prototype, and this was his failing: he missed the fundamental point that the good big submarine had infinitely more promise than the good little submarine. Where *Goubet I* did make her mark was in the popular imagination. The trials were well publicized, and probably *because* of her size the French public became keenly interested in her progress. The enthusiasm for Goubet's creation spilled over into submarine development generally.

This was a timely piece of good fortune for Admiral Aube, who had committed funds for a second submarine without waiting for delivery of the first. And here was a much more ambitious project. *Gymnote*, built by the gifted naval engineer Gustave Zédé, was about 60 feet long and equipped with a 55-horsepower motor run off electric batteries. While there were the usual difficulties with depth-keeping, *Gymnote* was a highly promising design, and Aube gave the go-ahead for another submarine along the same lines but very much larger. Gustave Zédé was killed by an explosion before his new submarine was completed and she was launched in 1893 bearing his name. Nearly 150 feet long and with a displacement of 266 tons the *Gustave Zédé* was the most advanced submarine to date anywhere—despite Holland's claims to the contrary. Aube suddenly discovered that he was not alone in his conviction that the underwater gunboat could and should become an integral part of the French fleet. And with France stroking boldly into the lead could other maritime nations afford not to give chase?

The two craft that gave France a temporary lead in submarine development. Above: The *Gymnote* in 1888, sixty feet long and powered by an electric motor. Right: The *Gustave Zédé* at the turn of the century, more than twice *Gymnote*'s length and also electrically powered

3. THE BIRTH OF THE MODERN SUBMARINE

In America, Holland was still hard at work, although very much a prophet without honour. Private inventors who lack private means are always in a precarious position, and John Holland's lonely struggle against indifference, obstruction, and sharp practice was made supportable only by his fervent conviction that he and he alone held the secret to underwater travel. Small wonder that Holland appeared, at least on occasion, to flirt with the dangerous belief that ill-disposed or at least stupid men were conspiring against him. His association with the Fenians came to an abrupt end in late 1883, when a number of them stole 'their' submarine and towed it to New Haven, Connecticut. Apparently they had finally lost patience with Holland's painstaking trials, which showed no signs of coming to an end. After making a few unsuccessful attempts to master the controls they gave up, and the *Fenian Ram* was abandoned. Holland was understandably furious, and never again had anything to do with the movement.

Having neither money nor influential friends, Holland was forced to quit the field and take a job as draughtsman with the Pneumatic Gun Company of New York. Before long, he managed to persuade some of his colleagues to finance another submarine venture, and with their aid he founded the Nautious Submarine Boat Company. In collaboration with an artillery officer, Captain Zalinski, Holland now constructed another submarine. The novelty of the 'Zalinski boat', as she was nicknamed, lay in a compressed air gun which threw out a charge of dynamite. This was an advance on the *Fenian Ram's* armament but a pale shadow of the Whitehead torpedo, although in the event this mattered little. As the submarine was sliding down the launching ways for her first trial in 1886 the ways collapsed and Holland could only watch as the wooden craft broke up against some piling. Nearly ten years would pass before he found the money to build another submarine.

In 1888, however, it must have seemed to Holland that he was finally on the brink of success. The Secretary of the Navy, William Whitney, was persuaded to hold an open competition for submarine design. Holland and Nordenfelt were among the entrants, but it was a hopeless task from the beginning because totally unrealistic performance figures were demanded. The Holland design was judged best but it could be seen even on paper to have no chance of meeting the requirements, and the matter was shelved. In 1893 a similar competition was held and again Holland won, but even then the Navy stalled for another two years before making an appropriation of $150,000. Again the contract was hedged around with impossible performance specifications, yet Holland had no choice but to try to fulfil them. As work progressed through 1896 it became increasingly apparent to him that he was building a white elephant. The Holland design had always been geared to produce a compact

Above: The *Peral*, built in 1888 by a Spanish naval lieutenant. The submarine caused a flurry of excitement and for a short time Peral was a national hero

Previous pages: The legendary *Holland*, completed in 1898 and finally purchased by the U.S. Navy in 1900. The small but superbly designed craft was the culmination of more than twenty years' dedicated work

and manoeuvrable submarine, yet the *Plunger* was 84 feet long. She had to have this bulk in order to accommodate the massive steam engine needed to provide great range and speed on the surface. But as had been amply demonstrated steam would provide only a short (and uncomfortable) run submerged, so the *Plunger* was equipped with an electric engine as well. It was not an impossible concept but it was too cumbersome for Holland's tastes. He saw that the submarine would fail and that his own chances might disappear forever, and he saw this with such clarity that he determined on bold, even reckless action. Leaving aside the *Plunger*, and ignoring all naval specifications, he designed another submarine and managed to get private backing for the venture. His idea was to present the navy with a *fait accompli* and gamble on their acceptance. At the beginning of 1898 he unveiled the submarine which has always been known simply as the *Holland*, and seemingly despite itself the U.S. navy was confronted with the first unqualified success in submarine history.

The *Holland* was little more than 50 feet in length, large enough to house a crew of five and one torpedo tube, but small enough to be extremely manoeuvrable and responsive to the controls her designer had laboured so many years to perfect. Holland retained the twin-propulsion system of the *Plunger*, but with an important difference: for surface power, rather than rely on steam, he substituted a newfangled gasoline engine of 45 horsepower. This gave the *Holland* a surface speed of 7 knots and a range of 1,000 miles, while the battery-powered electric motor provided a top speed of 5 knots with a 50-mile range. These were not impressive speeds but it was easy to see that they could be improved upon in subsequent models. The important things were that the boat ran easily on the surface, dived quickly, could fire a Whitehead torpedo submerged, and rose to the surface again on command. Enthusiastic reports began flooding into naval headquarters—reports from independent observers, government officials, naval personnel—but still the navy dragged its feet. This was all happening in the wake of the brief Spanish–American War, and naturally enough the opinion of Admiral Dewey was solicited. He stated bluntly that two enemy submarines would have made untenable his position in Manila Bay—where he had fifteen ships. This was a scarifying judgement because Spain might have had the two submarines Dewey spoke of. In 1888, fully ten years before this decisive action in the Philippines, a Spanish naval lieutenant, Isaac Peral, had built an electric-powered submarine that was every bit as promising as any contemporary models. Peral had then fallen out with his superiors and the matter was dropped. Was there not a lesson here? Finally, in April 1900, purchase was authorized. Holland received $150,000 and a commission for more submarines, while the untested *Plunger* was conveniently forgotten. Holland's tribulations were by no means over: he had been forced—again for financial reasons—to merge his interests in a new firm, the Electric Boat Company, and control over his invention had slipped forever from his grasp. Yet he had done enough to merit his rarely disputed title of 'father of the modern submarine'.

Despite Holland's breakthrough, as the new century dawned France still held a commanding lead in the field. In 1896 the Minister of Marine, like his American counterpart earlier, announced an open competition for submarine design, and he wanted something quite different from the type of craft already possessed by the navy. The *Gymnote* and *Gustave Zédé* had over the years undergone a number of modifications that greatly increased their stability, and a new submarine, the *Morse*, would incorporate these advances when she finally came off the stocks in 1899. Yet one great disadvantage remained. While their electric motors provided ample power for a submerged run, they did not have the endurance for useful surface work simply because the batteries needed frequent recharging and this could not be done at sea. The *Holland* enjoyed much more mobility by virtue of her gasoline engine, which not only provided a vastly greater range on the surface but could also be used to recharge the batteries. The advantage of employing twin-propulsion systems was overwhelming and would soon become, and long remain, universal. Lockroy, the Minister of Marine, wanted a boat that could make reasonably high speed on the surface over a great distance, and run submerged for the comparatively short stretch necessary to carry out a surprise

The French *Narval*, at dock and on manoeuvres. Like the *Holland*, she employed a twin-propulsion system, but with steam rather than gasoline for surface power

attack—a submersible torpedo-boat, in fact, very much the sort of thing that Nordenfelt had striven unsuccessfully for.

As a result of the competition the Laubeuf-designed *Narval* was laid down in 1898 and completed the following year. At the same time, 3,000 miles away, the rival *Holland* was undergoing her exhaustive trials. These two advanced craft differed in important respects. While both used electric motors submerged, the *Narval* employed steam power on the surface—the method Holland had abandoned with the *Plunger*. More important, the *Narval* was really two boats in one. She had an outer hull resembling that of a conventional torpedo-boat, and an inner hull along the traditional fish-like submarine lines. The crew and all the equipment were confined to the inner pressure-resistant hull while between the two were the ballast tanks. When the ballast tanks were empty the *Narval* rode high in the water and with the excellent sea-keeping characteristics of a surface torpedo-boat. She could make an impressive 11 knots and had a range of 500 miles. Underwater she could manage 8 knots for a short run and 5 knots over several hours. Again, as with the *Holland*, the surface engine could be used to recharge the batteries for the electric motor.

Both the *Narval*'s strength and weakness lay in the use of steam. At the turn of the century the internal combustion engine was in its infancy whereas the steam engine was highly advanced, and was indeed the only possible method of developing sufficient power for good surface performance. Set against this were the peculiar characteristics of steam engines which have already been described and which would always

make them unsatisfactory for submarine work—even where their application was restricted to surface propulsion. It took fully twenty minutes to shut down the engines and get the *Narval* underwater, and even then the lingering heat made things uncomfortable for the crew.

Where the *Narval* marked an unqualified advance, however, was in her double-hull construction. The French would be slow to lose faith in the uncompromising underwater boat of the *Gustave Zédé* variety (the *sousmarin* type) but it was the ocean-going submersible torpedo-boat that would hit naval warfare with so shattering an impact. Yet the double-hull concept had not originated with the *Narval*, nor indeed with a gunboat of any description. It had occurred first to an extraordinary young American named Simon Lake, who had been busying himself with submarine construction since the early nineties, alone and seemingly outside the mainstream of development. Like the Englishman Garrett before him, Lake was fascinated by the possibilities of underwater travel not underwater war. If Holland was poor he was not without influential friends, whereas Lake had neither money nor, given his aims, did he have the natural alliance with either warlike amateurs or imaginative naval experts.

In 1893, with a very little capital borrowed from relatives, he built what was probably the most unlikely-looking submarine since Bushnell's *Turtle*. The *Argonaut Jr* looked like an oversize sea captain's chest. Built of pine planking lined with canvas, she was flat-sided with a little hatch on top—and with wooden wheels on the bottom. The wheels were turned by a hand crank, and the idea was to take on sufficient ballast to sink to the bottom and then trundle along the sea-bed. Should anything interesting come into view the operator, in full diving gear, could simply step outside through a pressurized air lock, scoop it up, and return. The *Argonaut Jr* stands out in refreshing contrast to all the underwater engines of death that precede and follow her, and it is a pleasure to recount that she was as effective as she was enchanting: Lake and a companion spent many happy hours combing the bottom of New York Bay for oysters and clams.

As soon as he could get backing, Lake went on to build the *Argonaut*, a much larger submarine which he completed in 1897. The *Argonaut* was powered by a 30-horsepower gasoline engine, and this served both for surface and underwater propulsion—an awkward arrangement because gasoline engines need air, and this had to be provided either through a hose attached to a buoy on the surface or (later) a long funnel. Shortly after beginning trials with the *Argonaut*, Lake decided that he could improve her seaworthiness immeasurably by wrapping her round with a second skin, a superstructure in the shape of a conventional boat. The transformation was

Above Simon Lake poses with his first submarine, the tiny *Argonaut Jr*. Despite a rather comical appearance, the craft performed well

successful: with her ballast tanks empty the *Argonaut* rode the waves with ease; when they were filled she descended on an even keel—rather than diving like the *Holland*—and proceeded along at a modest depth with her air-intake pipe, or rudimentary schnorkel, poking out above the surface.

At this point Lake seems to have begun thinking along more traditional and less peaceful lines: he decided that the *Argonaut* would be ideal for clearing minefields, or, by corollary, for laying mines, and he too began the thankless task of lobbying the U.S. navy for contracts. Where Holland encountered evasion and delay Lake met with blunt refusal, and after several rebuffs he began to look overseas for customers. Nearly twenty years later this inventor casually remarked—as though it were a truism of the day—that 'Americans invent and the Europeans develop'. To the modern observer this complaint has a fantastical quality: it is remarkable how (supposed) national characteristics can be so quickly and so completely exchanged.

The hesitancy, the extreme caution in American official circles over pursuing a development in which individual Americans were in the forefront is strange enough. What is truly astonishing, however, is how the story of submarines has unfolded thus far with scarcely a mention of the two nations whose destinies were inextricably linked with the new device: Great Britain and Germany. During the final decades of the nineteenth century the submarine had become a weapon of at least *potential* menace. If the claims of its devotees were not to be discounted altogether the invisible torpedo-boat might revolutionize maritime war. Yet as late as 1900 the greatest of navies affected not to notice; several more years were to elapse before interest was aroused in that quarter from which the menace would be ruthlessly confirmed. How could this be true? Why and how did this state of affairs change so rapidly and decisively?

In the first place, the British naval establishment had not so much ignored recent developments as it had disparaged them. The reasons for this were a perilous mixture of stupidity and wishful thinking. There were those who blithely ignored the growing weight of evidence about submarine performance for no better reason than that it was inconceivable for tiny experimental craft to challenge the might of the Royal Navy. If inferior powers wanted to waste time and money in self-deception they were welcome to do so. Then there was another view, much less simple-minded, which in practical terms came down to the same thing. Suppose the submarine really were—or might become—formidable. To whose advantage would it be? Clearly not to Britain's, as St Vincent had pointed out with unanswerable logic a century before. Practically every person involved in submarine experiment had at one time or another boasted that his new invention would redress the imbalance

Overleaf: The *Argonaut*. Lake had the novel idea of incorporating wheels, so that his submarines could move crablike along the sea bed. Note the other submarine under construction behind the *Argonaut*: this is Holland's unlamented *Plunger*

53

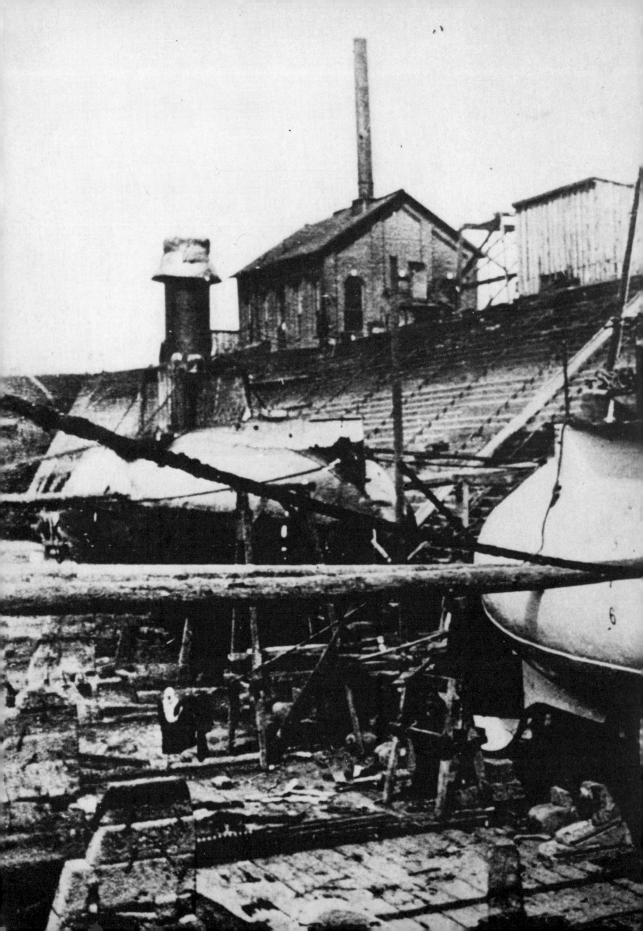

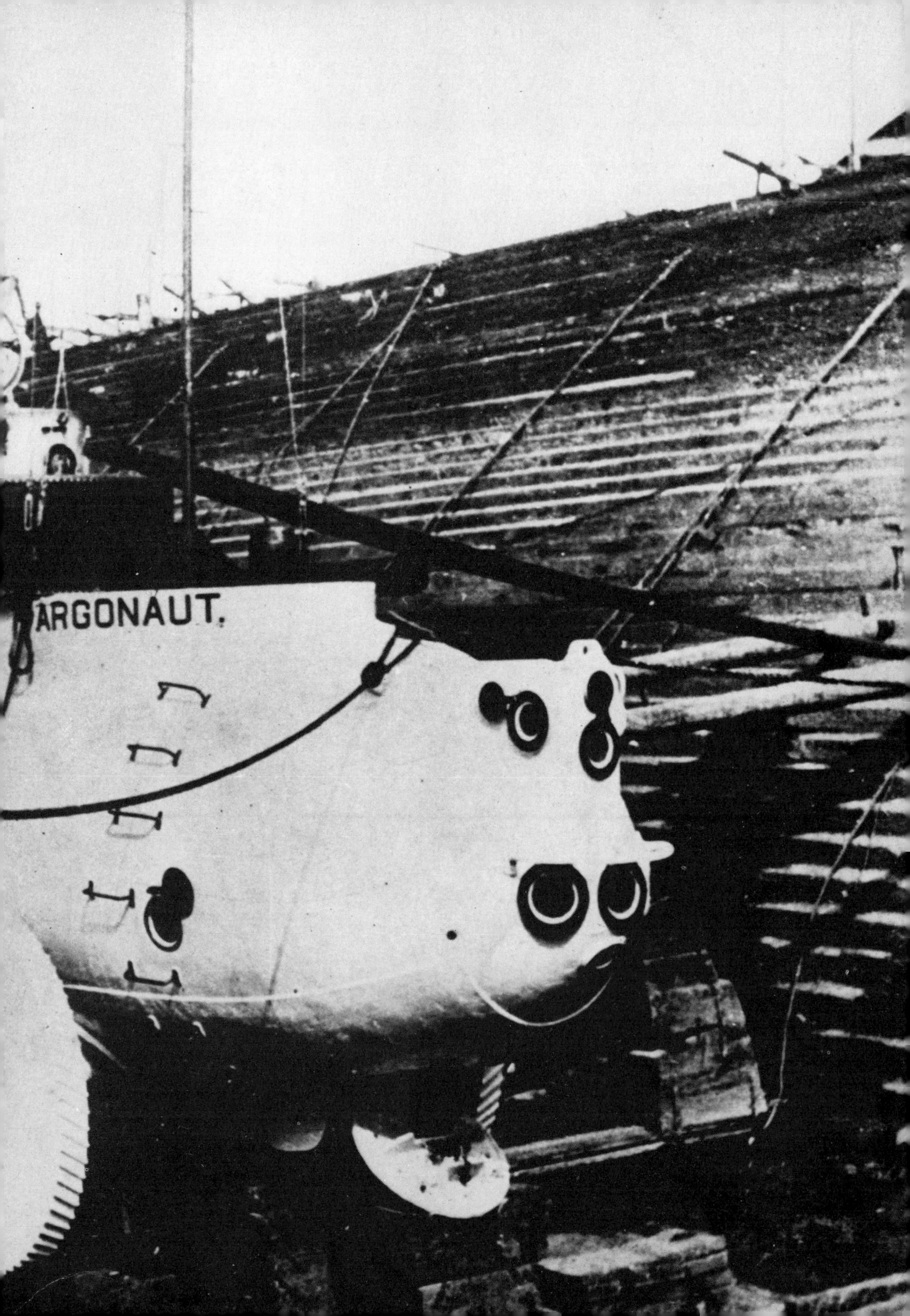
ARGONAUT.

between those who ruled the waves and those who did not. This was a sentiment guaranteed to send shivers up and down Admiralty spines. The Royal Navy was not only incomparably the greatest, it was greater than any plausible combination of navies that might be brought against it. Because of Britain's unique position in the world—a small industrialized island dependent for its livelihood upon trade and in particular upon the resources of a far-flung empire—it was imperative that this overwhelming naval superiority be maintained. The submarine could not possibly be of benefit to a superior navy since it threatened the pre-eminence of capital ships. Effective submarines would alter the *status quo* by devaluing existing warships, so they were by definition the weapon of the inferior power. It was therefore a logical absurdity for Britain to touch them, and if she did, her rivals would be quick to see the flaw. Worse, they would smell fear. The submarine must be contemptuously dismissed, in which case others might lose interest in it. This was not quite so ostrich-like as it may appear. Britain's influence on the naval strategy of other maritime nations was profound; it was exceeded only by British estimates of that influence. Finally, if this unwelcome intruder could not be driven away by indifference and scorn, it might be swept away by a burst of moral indignation. The submarine was clearly a barbarous device, in the splendid phrase of Admiral A. K. Wilson, 'underhand, unfair, and damned un-English'. Its use in warfare should be prohibited.

This policy, if it can be called a policy, was bound to prove unsatisfactory, and for his part 'Tug' Wilson was merely parroting the time-honoured hypocrisy reserved for new methods of fighting by those who are proficient in the old. Something would have to be done, and in the year 1900 a swelling chorus began calling for immediate action. The French were building submarines at an alarming rate, and if war with France had been narrowly averted over Fashoda in 1898 it might not be averted the next time. The *Gustave Zédé* had 'torpedoed' the battleship *Magenta* during manoeuvres in 1898, and the French were making no secret of the fact that in submarines they felt they had the measure of the Royal Navy. By 1900 fourteen submarines were either in service or on the stocks, and it was resolved to expand this flotilla to thirty-eight as quickly as possible. Even accepting the argument about the submarine being the weapon of the inferior power, what guarantee was there that such a power when strengthened by any number of submarines would *remain* inferior?

In November 1900 the Admiralty ordered five submarines from the Electric Boat Company. It was a convenient way to begin, but the purpose was not to add a submarine arm to the Royal Navy by simple purchase. The submarine was still generally considered unnecessary and unsuitable for British

Right: The submarine commander watches his prey in this artist's impression of French naval manoeuvres in the early 1900s. The success claimed for submarines in such exercises was impressive and prompted British entry into the field

purposes, but it was imperative to develop means of countering their threat. It would therefore be appropriate to find out more about them, and it was sensibly decided to buy the best on the market. In fact once having decided to act the Admiralty scarcely put a foot wrong. Rather than await delivery of the new Hollands (the U.S. navy already had five on order) it was arranged that they be built in England by Vickers, under American guidance. This provided British designers and engineers with an opportunity to absorb very quickly the lessons of twenty painstaking years. They seized it with alacrity, and before the Holland boats were completed work was forging ahead on a vastly improved design, the *AI*. This A class was much larger than the Holland and equipped with a 500-horsepower Wolsley engine. Very soon both types were giving a good account of themselves in manoeuvres—in marked contrast to anti-submarine devices employed against them—and there was a welcome decline in the specious rhetoric about inferior and superior powers. The submarine had come to stay and the British navy was assuming its 'rightful' position in the forefront of developments.

What of Imperial Germany? As early as 1892 the navy had taken delivery of two submarines built to the Nordenfelt design, but these had been judged outright failures and the idea not worth pursuing. As Admiral von Tirpitz saw it, the submarine was a red herring, a flimsy device which perhaps offered some measure of coastal defence but had nothing whatever to do with the balance of sea power. Germany had little coast to defend, and Tirpitz would brook no distraction from the herculean task of building up the High Seas Fleet. There the matter lay for a dozen years, and even Britain's belated entry into this branch of the arms race made no impression. Britain, after all, had much coast to defend, and that she had opted for submarines might well be taken as a back-handed compliment to the rising stature of the German navy.

The French, in the meantime, had finally decided in favour of the Narval-type submersible, although they retained the all-electric *sousmarins* for coastal defence. But they were having chronic difficulties with gasoline engines, which forced them time and again to revert to steam. This technical hitch, combined with the radical shift in strategic thinking brought about by Anglo-French *entente*, meant that France began to lose her carefully built up lead in submarine development.

The Americans, who had been second only to France at the turn of the century, were slipping badly behind. The U.S. navy saw no virtue in submarines beyond a limited use in coastal defence—scarcely a pressing concern given America's relative isolation—and in the years leading up to 1914 it was content to add Hollands at a desultory rate. Yet American submarines were still making their presence felt in the navies of the world.

One of the original Holland
class submarines built by
Vickers for the Royal Navy.
The Hollands quickly gave way
to the British designed A class

Japan purchased several Hollands after the outbreak of war
with Russia in 1904, although they were not completed in time
to see action. Russia too bought a Holland, as well as Simon
Lake's new submarine, the *Protector*. For the remaining pre-
war years these American designs were the nucleus of the
expanding submarine flotillas of both powers. Russia, however,
had unwittingly made a move of profound significance. In 1904
she ordered three submarines from Krupp-Germania, submarines based on the advanced French designs.

It suddenly dawned on the German navy that the submarine
might now be a practical proposition. These new submarines
that were being laid down for Russia were true overseas boats.
They were powerful and designed to travel long distances, and

The British submarine *A1*, based on the Holland design but with better performance from a much more powerful engine. The *A1* was accidently rammed in 1904 and sank, killing eleven men

Left: The first U-boat, *U1*, in
commission with the German
navy by the end of 1906

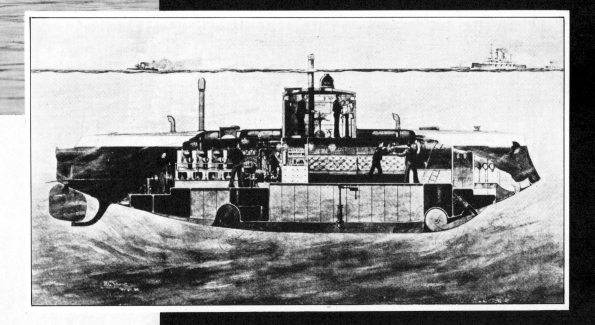

Above: Lake's *Protector*,
which was purchased by the
Russian navy. Note the
retractable wheels. Left: The
British submarine *B1* passes
Nelson's *Victory* in 1905

with their double-hull construction and great buoyancy they were clearly seaworthy. These were no mere adjuncts to coastal defence; they had potential for *offence*. This striking fact about French submersibles might well have occurred to the Germans some years earlier, since the French had never disguised their belief that large submarines could play an offensive role. In any case having taken the point the Germans moved swiftly. By the end of 1906 the navy had taken delivery of its first *Unterseeboot, UI,* from Krupp-Germania, and more and larger submarines were in the pipeline.

During the final years leading up to world war, submarines got bigger and better and they proliferated. What is of greater importance is the change—or lack of it—in naval thinking that accompanied the adoption of submarines by the great navies. From the modern vantage point it seems crystal clear that the submarine was bound to play a tremendously important part in the coming struggle. This would have been the case even if war had come several years earlier than it did. Yet while most contemporary strategists were agreed that the new weapon was an important one, its true significance proved remarkably elusive. The Royal Navy still viewed submarines with mixed feelings, although this did not hold back a determined building programme. The B class gave way to the C, still essentially a Holland coastal submarine, but the D class (developed from 1906) marked an enormous advance. These submarines displaced nearly 500 tons (almost double the Bs and Cs), they were double-hulled like the French submersibles with the consequent improvement in sea-keeping characteristics, and they had experimental diesel engines. In 1912 the first E class submarines went into commission, and by 1914 the Royal Navy had eleven of this new type. The Es had a surface displacement of about 700 tons and were equipped with four 18-inch torpedo tubes (two fore and two aft). They could make 15–16 knots on the surface, and nearly 10 knots submerged, and had a useful range of 1,500 miles (in other words they could travel double that distance). These D and E classes were first-class ocean-going warships, but it was not at all clear what their purpose was. Like the French, the British strove to integrate their submarines with conventional fleet movements, with only partial success because submarines could not move fast enough even on the surface to keep up with conventional warships. Nor would they stand up to the roughest weather conditions. To minds conditioned by the Dreadnought Age the submarine was a puny thing, slow, unreliable, and dangerous to its crew. This latter point had great substance to it. Beginning in 1904 British submarines started taking a fearful toll of lives. In that year the *AI* was rammed by S.S. *Berwick Castle* during manoeuvres and took eleven men to the bottom. The next year a similar number perished in an explosion on *A5*. Over the next few years more

64

With the D class (*D1* below and *D4* bottom) British submarines became seaworthy warships. They were large, well armed, and powered by experimental diesel engines collisions and explosions added regularly to this total.

The French too were having difficulties in co-ordinating their overseas submarines with the rest of the fleet. Their engine troubles were not solved by the switch from gasoline to heavy oil, and they were experiencing their share of fatal accidents. Like the British they continued to build steadily but without the resolution that could only be provided by clear purpose, and when war finally came the French would find that their pioneering work paid no dividends at all.

It might be supposed that Germany, having come into the picture after everyone else, would throw everything into submarine development and race to the front. In fact attitudes there were not strikingly different from those in Britain and France, although if Germany was in a sense drifting she at least was drifting in the right direction. From 1907 onwards U-boats were steadily added to the navy, although not as a result of any crash building programme. By accident as much as by design, however, these U-boats were tailor-made for what would emerge in warfare as Germany's strategic requirements. Coastal defence was not an obsession, and the German navy therefore avoided the agonized debate over the relative merits of coastal and overseas boats and went unhesitatingly for the latter. Again, having started late, the Germans were able to avoid most of the mistakes that had plagued and were plaguing others: they were in a position to pick and choose among rival concepts. They started with a good French design and improved upon it immediately. They rightly ignored steam power and (again rightly) decided that gasoline engines were too dangerous because the fumes were at once explosive and toxic. They began with heavy oil (paraffin) and then followed the British lead with diesel engines. Here they went one better, and the diesel engines that appeared in U-boats from 1913 were in a class by themselves. So too were U-boat periscopes. Everyone had some sort of periscope by this time, but with her great tradition in optical equipment Germany moved easily to the front in this vital development.

Taken all in all the successive classes of U-boat that came into service in the final pre-war years were as good as the British Es and in some respects better. Their surface and submerged speeds were equivalent but the U-boats could, at reduced speed, range a thousand miles further afield. They were equipped with 19·7-inch torpedoes and these were not only larger than British torpedoes but they worked better. Of overriding importance is the fact that by the time war broke out almost all Germany's U-boats were capable of this sort of performance. The British and French between them possessed six or seven times as many submarines, but the vast majority of these were either obsolete or obsolescent. There could be no comparison at all between, say, the B and C class British submarines and U-boats. The

The 700-ton E class (*E6* below in 1913) would play the major role in British submarine campaigns during the coming war. The 1,270-ton *Nautilus* (bottom) was designed in 1912 but not completed till near the end of the First World War. She was intended for fleet operations but did not see action

vital statistic is that the twenty-odd U-boats in service by 1914 outnumbered E types by two to one.

Yet for all this—and there can be no better example of the shrewd move shrewdly timed—the Germans were not following any sinister master plan, they were not consciously developing 'the ultimate weapon'. They were merely getting into the swim with everybody else, and they built the type of submarine they did for the logical reason that it was the only one that could be of any use to them. Because of their stealth U-boats would be ideal for reconnaissance, for warding off a blockade of the North Sea ports, and they might well be valuable in any general action. The German fleet, for all its strength, was markedly inferior to the British fleet, and anything that could narrow the gap was welcome. As Europe hurtled towards war, Germany was not looking to the submarine for her salvation any more than Britain was looking to it for her ruin.

On 4 August 1914 Great Britain declared war on Germany. On 5 August two British submarines accompanied a small British force sailing east out of Harwich. At the same time German U-boats were concentrated in the Heligoland Bight, where a British attack was considered imminent.

Two views of the U-boat interior. In less than twenty years the submarine had moved from infancy to maturity—and, as these U-boats would amply demonstrate, right to the centre of naval power

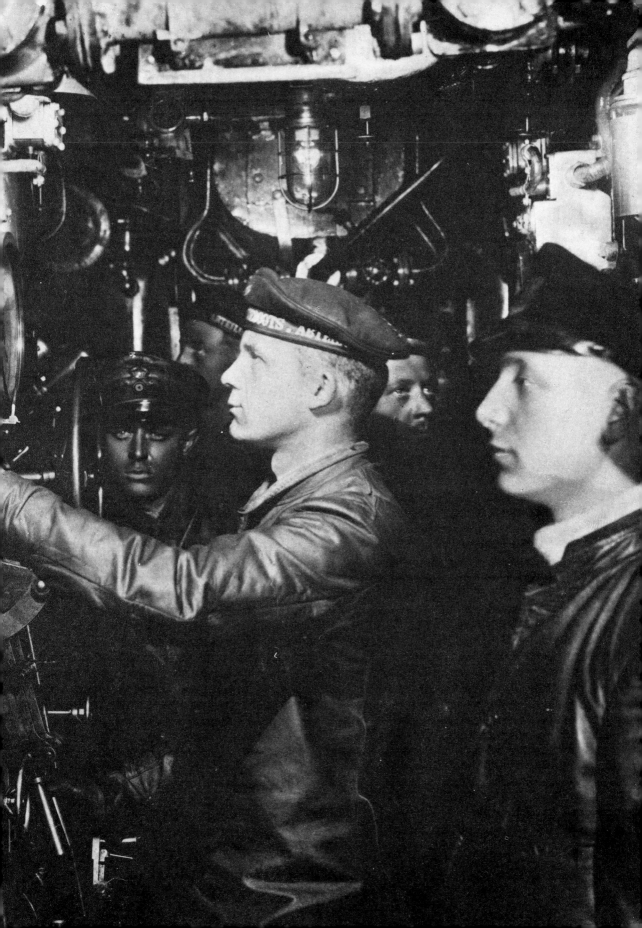

4. THE FIRST RECKONING

Germany's U-boat campaign against commerce (and Britain's attempt to foil it) is the most salient feature of naval operations during the First World War, and in general terms it is very well known. Germany tried to force Britain out of the war by killing her overseas trade and thereby bringing on industrial collapse and outright starvation. The employment of submarines against merchant shipping was the chief—in practical terms the sole—means to that end. The policy came within a whisker of success, but in the end proved ruinous to the German cause because it was instrumental in bringing the United States into the war on the Allied side. To understand how this came about, how it was that a new and untried weapon played such a dominant—almost decisive—role in a mighty war, it is essential to grasp the German and British plans of action when hostilities commenced.

Put briefly, the Germans intended to hold against the Russians in the east while delivering a knockout blow against the French in the west; having dispatched the French they would turn their main thrust against the Russians, who could not hope to stand before it. The war would be finished almost as soon as it began. To the eleventh hour and beyond it was fervently hoped that the British would have the sense to stay out of it, but when this hope died it made no difference to the grand strategy. The newly constructed German battle fleet was spoiling for the chance to prove itself, and it could scarcely have a more testing opponent. The British navy was much stronger and it certainly had the weight of prestige and experience, but this might prove to be a dead weight. In any case Britain had much more to lose in a naval showdown since all her fortunes rested squarely on sea power. Britain *had* to have command of the seas in order to survive, whereas Germany could at a pinch concede freedom of the seas and still defeat the armies ranged against her, thereby winning the war.

On 4 August 1914, however, the German navy was in no mood to concede victory to the British navy, although it freely conceded superiority. The plan was for the High Seas Fleet to wait patiently in its well-defended corner of the Heligoland Bight. It was taken for fact that the British, who knew exactly where the German fleet was, would immediately move in for the kill, and they might well do so before there was a declaration of war. They would come sweeping across the North Sea, blockade the Heligoland Bight, and dare the High Seas Fleet to sally forth. If the Germans obliged, their navy would be shattered; if they remained in the safety of their lair, they would concede mastery of the seas. To counter this *supposed* British strategy the Germans adopted the only plan that made sense. They would harass the blockading forces at every opportunity—submarines might be ideal for this purpose—and when these guerilla tactics succeeded in cutting the British fleet

Previous pages: A U-boat crew man the gun in heavy seas. The gun made it possible to attack small vessels which were not worth wasting a torpedo on

Above and right: The shattering impact of U-boat warfare on British commerce

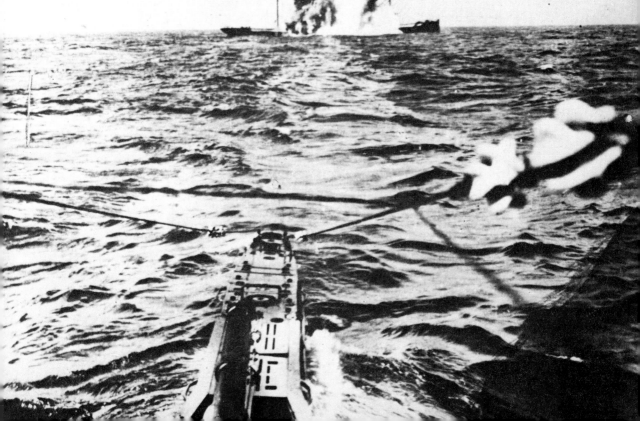

down to manageable size, then and only then would the main German force come to battle. Through the long daylight hours of 5 August the U-boats sat in a watching circle around Heligoland but the British did not come.

Seen through British eyes the coming war looked quite different. The Germans were bent on destroying the hallowed 'balance of power' on the Continent, while at the same time they were striving with might and main to challenge Britain's naval supremacy: they were trying to succeed where Napoleon had failed, and they would be defeated in the same way. The British army would aid its European allies while the Royal Navy would sooner or later destroy Germany's capacity to make war. The fleet would protect England from invasion and allow her vital commerce to proceed undisturbed. At the same time it would deny Germany use of the seas—for either military or commercial purposes—which to an industrialized trading nation would prove crippling. It would do this either by defeating the German fleet in a general action (the most satisfying manner) or by bottling it up in home waters if it refused to fight. Whichever way, British shipping would be undisturbed and German shipping would be swept from the seas.

Thus far the Germans had read British intentions correctly, and that is why on 5 August they were scanning the horizon for British warships. What they did not know, or did not guess, was that the Royal Navy was genuinely alarmed at the prospect of sending its fleet into waters infested with torpedo-boats and submarines. It would blockade the Germans from afar, sealing off the exits from the North Sea. There would be sorties into disputed waters—again the submarine looked promising for this role—but the British would wait for the enemy to come to them, which, just as in the case of a close blockade, he would be forced to do or concede defeat. The Grand Fleet was positioned to cover the northern exit between Scotland and Norway, while the Channel Fleet blockaded the English Channel from the east. The German navy was therefore as powerless as it would be under close blockade, and once it realized that fact, pride alone would force it to come out fighting. The sooner this happened the better since annihilation at sea would surely force Germany to rethink its absurd posturing. Should German militarists remain obdurate they would see their proud nation slowly strangled. Nothing their vaunted army achieved would save them. They would find, as Napoleon had found before them, that to be denied absolutely the commerce of the seas meant death, as surely as to be deprived of air. At 11 p.m. on 4 August all ships in the Royal Navy received the signal to commence hostilities against Germany. The fleets were in position and four hours later two of the new long-range submarines, *E6* and *E8*, were moving with a small flotilla

Two arms of the Royal Navy during the war. Top: A cruiser squadron in close formation. Above: *E20*, which was sunk by a U-boat in the Sea of Marmara in 1915

towards Heligoland. The aim was to see what the Germans were up to and it might well provide an opportunity to draw first blood.

As the first day of the war dragged on uneventfully the Germans racked their brains for an explanation. Where were the enemy warships? It was a safe bet that the Channel Fleet was staying put to cover troop landings in France, but where was the mighty Grand Fleet? It must be setting up its blockade further out than anticipated, perhaps as much as two or three hundred miles out from Heligoland. Showing admirable and perhaps surprising flexibility, the Germans immediately leapt to the offensive. At dawn on the 6th, ten U-boats struck out to the north-west in search of the enemy. This was no mere reconnaissance mission, it was an audacious thrust aimed at sinking as many battleships as possible and thereby shattering the confidence of the British navy. One of the U-boats turned back with engine trouble, but the others pushed on into heavy fog. The Grand Fleet again was not where it was supposed to be and the submarines pushed further north. By the 8th they were as far north as the Orkneys, and here, at last, the enemy came into view. The Grand Fleet was patrolling between Scotland and Norway and a detachment of three battleships was engaging in target practice some distance from the main body of the fleet. *U15* saw them and managed to fire a torpedo at the *Monarch*. It narrowly missed. The next day, having turned back for home, the U-boats ran smack into advance cruisers of the Grand Fleet. The submarines were virtually blind in the choppy seas and heavy mist but one of them was spotted by the cruiser *Birmingham*. *U15* was rammed twice and sank with all her crew, while her companion U-boats sailed on, unaware that their quarry was immediately at hand. On the same day, the 9th, *U13* disappeared for reasons unknown, and by the 11th the remaining U-boats were safely home.

Two submarines lost for no gain—not even information about the Grand Fleet's location—was scarcely a victory. Yet this inconclusive mission was of profound importance for both sides. The Germans now knew for sure what they had only suspected before, that in the U-boats they had a weapon of startling potency: here was a warship that could operate alone and unsupported at long range in enemy waters. Over the next few weeks these U-boat patrols were stepped up, and they dared to go as far as the English coast. These excursions, harmless as they were for the first few weeks, gave the Royal Navy a terrible fright. Scapa Flow, which had become the Grand Fleet's operational base as soon as war broke out, was by some astonishing piece of carelessness totally undefended. What terrible mayhem could a pack of U-boats spread if they got loose in there while the fleet was at rest?

Men aboard the British ships began to experience the most unpleasant side effect of submarine warfare, something that had been only vaguely glimpsed by the most far-sighted before the war: they became jittery. The depths below them now contained an unseen menace, and it could attack them at any time from any direction. With great apprehension they scanned the seas and sometimes they saw submarines that were not there at all. When a genuine sighting occurred it was very likely that the same intruder would be seen in many different places at once. Anyone who has experienced a shark alert on a public beach will know how menacing every rock and every shadow suddenly becomes. And of course one of those dark shapes that somebody sees probably is a shark. Midway through the afternoon of 5 September, H.M.S. *Pathfinder* was patrolling off

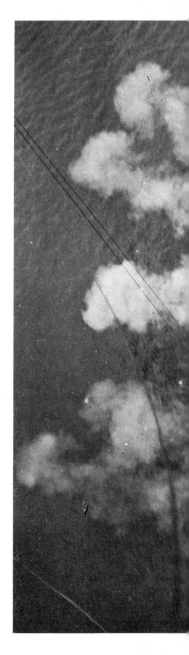

The cruiser *Birmingham* fires a salvo. She had the distinction of sinking the first U-boat of the war, on 9 August 1914

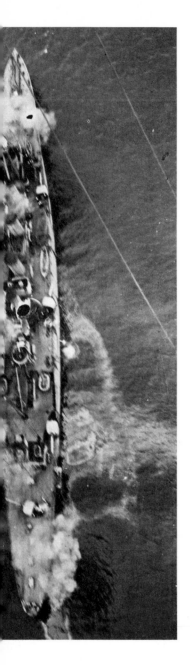

St Abb's Head, just outside the entrance to the Firth of Forth. Without warning she was struck by a torpedo, her forward magazine blew up and she sank almost immediately, taking more than 250 men with her. *U21*, under Lieutenant-Commander Otto Hersing, had become the first submarine to sink a warship since the *Hunley* half a century before, and she had not committed suicide in doing so.

Shortly after dawn on 22 September the three antiquated cruisers *Aboukir*, *Hogue*, and *Cressy* were moving slowly, in a straight line, some twenty miles off the Dutch coast. *U9*, an old pre-diesel U-boat which had been forced to turn back from the initial foray with engine trouble, lay directly in their path. This was pure accident because Lieutenant Otto Weddigen's U-boat was well off course as a result of a faulty gyro compass. Weddigen had been forced to spend the previous night on the bottom, and had spotted the cruisers in the distance after bringing *U9* back to the surface in order to recharge her batteries. For the British cruisers it was the most unfortunate of accidents. Oblivious to any danger they came straight on, abreast and two miles apart. At 6.20 the *Aboukir*, which was in the centre, was hit on the starboard side from a range of 500 yards. The force of the blow stopped her almost in her tracks, and she began to list heavily. Thinking that the *Aboukir* had struck a mine, the other ships moved in to the rescue. Both lowered boats and began picking up survivors as the *Aboukir* began to roll over and sink. At 6.55 tremendous explosions rocked the *Hogue* as two torpedoes found their mark. *U9* was now breaking surface very close to her second victim and in vain the *Hogue* fired round after round at her. By 7.05 both ships were gone, but the *Cressy* was still frantically picking up survivors. A few minutes later the U-boat's periscope was sighted, and the *Cressy* finally decided to run for it. She was scarcely under way when the first of two torpedoes struck home. The second, moments later, sent her to the bottom. In the space of an hour three 12,000-ton warships had fallen to one obsolescent submarine, with the loss of more than 1,300 officers and men. Weddigen cautiously picked his way back to Germany and a hero's welcome. The British were stunned.

Meanwhile, the British submarine flotilla, under Commodore Keyes, was busily patrolling the Heligoland Bight, but so far without the sort of tangible success achieved by the U-boats. The submarines were managing to keep fairly close tabs on enemy movements, but on the one occasion that a submarine came within range of a cruiser the torpedo ran right under its target. Finally on 13 September *E9* sank the light cruiser *Hela* just south of Heligoland. This would not have been very significant had the Germans not reacted in the same panicky way as their English counterparts. They decided thenceforth to exercise their fleet in the Baltic rather than the North Sea.

The victors: *U9* (right) and her commander, Otto Weddigen surrounded by his crew. The vanquished: the cruisers *Hogue* (left) and *Aboukir* (bottom left), and an artist's impression of British pluck in the face of disaster

This was a great nuisance, but it was as nothing compared to the inconvenience a few U-boats were causing the Royal Navy. U-boats appeared in the Firth of Forth, in the English Channel, and *U9* sank yet another cruiser, H.M.S. *Hawke*, which was on the northern patrol. Worse, *U9* and *U17* were seen reconnoitring the approaches to Scapa Flow. The blockade line was pushed even further north, clear out of the North Sea to cover the stretch between Scotland and Iceland. The Grand Fleet rushed out of Scapa Flow and fled to the supposed safety of northern Ireland and eastern Scotland. If this was not panic it was unseemly haste, and taken together with Germany's abrupt decision not to exercise in the North Sea it shows how the conduct of naval warfare had been transformed in a way that would have seemed fantastic little more than two months before. A handful of submarines had sent two mighty fleets scurrying for cover. Was the day of the battleship over? Was the submarine the new arbiter of sea power?

In fact both sides, and in particular the British, were greatly over-estimating the submarine threat to their battle fleets. As events would show, the submarine had only a subsidiary role to play in the contested waters of the North Sea. Neither side came anywhere near accomplishing with submarines what it had hoped for in the early stages of the war. Despite claiming the occasional warship the U-boat campaign of attrition did not reduce the Grand Fleet to the proportions of the High Seas Fleet and it never looked like doing so. The Grand Fleet could only be seriously weakened by cutting down its preponderance of dreadnoughts, and throughout the war U-boats did not manage even to hit, let alone sink, one of them. Nor, despite repeated attempts, did they succeed in luring detached portions of the enemy fleet into traps where the main German force could annihilate them. Furthermore, in the one great naval engagement of the war, the Battle of Jutland in May 1916, the U-boat played a negligible part.

The British viewed the submarine as an aid to coastal defence, and hoped it would be useful for reconnaissance and patrol. In its defensive role the submarine proved a stark failure: German warships raided the east coast of England numerous times and not once were they intercepted or even seen by the defending submarines. Their efforts were better rewarded in the reconnaissance field but they were not of great consequence. Before the Battle of Jutland submarine patrols consistently missed sorties by the High Seas Fleet and while much heavier patrolling corrected this fault from then on, the information never enabled the Grand Fleet to come to grips with its foe. Nor, despite continuous improvement in performance and sea-keeping characteristics, could even the most advanced submarines move quickly enough to close with enemy warships.

Below: Max Horton, commander of *E9* which drew first blood for the British by sinking the German cruiser *Hela* on 13 September 1914

Right: *E9* returns to harbour covered in ice, after sinking a German destroyer. She also played a distinguished role in the Baltic campaign

They failed abysmally to perform any of the tasks assigned to them at Jutland.

The reason the submarine proved disappointing in these respects is that it was being asked to do things for which it was not equipped. The submarine is not a conventional warship, and the wary fencing that was going on between great fleets in the North Sea was a conventional war. The submarine's great virtue is that it can penetrate enemy waters, lurk unseen, and then destroy ships that are unlucky enough to come within range. It is the ultimate bushwhacker. Submarines of the First World War had sufficient endurance to go anywhere they wanted, and to stay there just about as long as they wanted with near impunity. Anti-submarine devices were crude, and while they improved under the stimulus of war they could not hope to deal convincingly with an enemy that could not be seen and could not be flushed out into the open. Where the submarine did score it was almost invariably as a lone guerilla in hostile waters but, as has been seen, its early success led to great caution in the movements of capital ships. Steaming at full speed with frequent zigzags, and screened constantly by destroyers, the big ships could fall to submarines only if they were extremely unlucky. The submarine severely restricted movement but it did so to both sides, and it tipped the scales neither one way nor the other. The struggle for the North Sea, however, was not the only testing ground for the new weapon.

From one direction the Royal Navy could not blockade Germany. It could make sure that the Germans did not get out of the Baltic to the north, but it was impossible to prevent them from treating the Baltic as a German lake. The inferior Russian navy could not hinder the High Seas Fleet in its exercises, nor could it halt the vital trade with neutral Sweden, which provided Germany with iron ore. Here at least were limits on British sea power, and here was precisely the situation for which the submarine might have been invented: a limited stretch of water where the enemy was supreme and where he needed to be able to move freely and with confidence. There was one great snag however. Entering the Baltic is a fairly tricky business under any circumstances and it is almost impossible when someone is trying to stop you. The Sound is narrow and the German patrols were more than adequate. Submarines could not simply run the gauntlet submerged because in places the water is too shallow.

Nevertheless it was decided to risk it, and in mid-October 1914 three British submarines set out. *E11* was forced back but somehow *E1* and *E9* managed to dodge minefields, searchlights, dense merchant traffic, and heavy German patrols that were alerted to the menace. Later in the war *E1* and *E9* were joined by other submarines, and together they gave German shipping a hellish nightmare. Operating from Russian bases, they swept the Baltic end to end, and while the High Seas Fleet emerged unscathed, warships operating off the Eastern Front did not. Many were sunk and many more damaged, and a heavy toll was taken of merchantmen transporting iron ore. The campaign ended on a depressing note from the British standpoint, but that was from no failing of the submarines or their brave crews. With the Treaty of Brest-Litovsk in March 1918 the new Bolshevik regime agreed to surrender the British submarines to the Germans. Without bases or supplies, and with no chance whatever of getting out the way they came in, the submarines were helpless. They were scuttled and the crews made their way to safety overland.

If it was dangerous to send submarines into the Baltic it was little short of foolhardy to send them through the Dardanelles, yet here again British submarines performed astonishing feats. In the first month of the war two German warships which were trapped in the Mediterranean fled through the Dardanelles into the Sea of Marmara, while an Allied fleet set up watch outside the Straits to make sure that they stayed there. On the last day of October 1914 Turkey came into the war against the Allies, and the Dardanelles suddenly assumed much greater importance. In March 1915 an attempt to break through the Straits was repulsed, and the fateful decision was taken to mount an overland assault on Gallipoli. This is where submarines came into it. The previous December one of the old coastal

Right: *B11* makes good her escape after dealing a mortal blow to the Turkish battleship *Messoudieh*, 13 December 1914

82

types, a few of which had been stationed in the Mediterranean before the war, had ventured into the heavily defended Straits. Against all the odds *B11* had sunk the Turkish battleship *Messoudieh*. Now if it were possible for a few of the larger E types to slip right through the Straits into the Sea of Marmara it would help the Allied campaign on the peninsula tremendously, because the principal route for supplying the Turkish defenders was by water from Constantinople. The idea bordered on the absurd because the Straits were guarded by shore batteries; they were mined, netted, and patrolled, and they are in any case extremely treacherous. Furthermore, in the unlikely event of surviving all that and getting into the Sea of Marmara a submarine would be absolutely on its own: there were no friendly bases as there were in the Baltic, and so at the end of a patrol it would be necessary to come back down the Straits. But the prize outweighed the risks and it was decided to try.

On 14 April *E15* started up the Straits, ran aground, and

The Allied submarine campaign in the Sea of Marmara was a spectacular success. Left: *E2*, one of nine British submarines involved. Below: Turkish victims of *E11* during the most successful patrol of all in August 1915

was destroyed by gunfire. Ten days later the Australian *AE2* managed to scrape through but fell to a torpedo-boat very shortly after. But *E14*, following, not only got into the Sea of Marmara but came out again three weeks later, having cut a wide swath through Turkish shipping and notably sinking a loaded troopship. *E11* followed on and scored even more heavily, and so it continued until the Gallipoli campaign was abandoned in December. There were casualties on the Allied side but the achievement was truly extraordinary. Scores of Turkish ships— including another battleship—were sent to the bottom; the sea communications between Constantinople and Gallipoli were almost completely severed; troops marching along the shore road were shelled; military targets came under fire; on one occasion Lieutenant D'Oyly Hughes of *E11* swam ashore and planted explosives on a railway bridge. Rarely can a nation at war have suffered such depredations at the hands of a small number of determined foes in its midst.

Understandably, the Turks were desperate to obtain some means of combating the marauders, but in the absence of really effective anti-submarine devices there was little they could do. They appealed to their German allies for naval help and they got it, although this had no direct effect on the grim state of affairs in the Sea of Marmara. The Germans dispatched one of their advanced U-boats to the Aegean. After the long run from Kiel right round the British Isles and through the Straits of Gibraltar *U21* arrived at the Dardanelles towards the end of May 1915. Within two days she sank the battleships *Triumph* and *Majestic* and thereby put an abrupt halt to Allied freedom of movement in the approaches. This was an important, arguably decisive, victory and of far greater consequence than the random sinking of the odd stray warship in the North Sea. In May 1915, however, it was not by sinking British battleships that the U-boat was making a name for itself. On the afternoon of the 7th, while *U21* was pushing steadily towards the Dardanelles, *U20* put a torpedo into the side of the Cunard liner *Lusitania*, eight miles off the Irish coast.

Germany's decision to employ U-boats as commerce raiders must rank as the most important event in the First World War—by far. Its significance is even wider than that for it marked the eclipse of a very old and cherished tradition in warfare between civilized states: it ended once and for all the distinction between combatant and civilian. Often the bomber aeroplane is cited in this context but the 'credit' belongs to the submarine. Before turning to the dreary catalogue of destruction, and the frantic attempts to halt the carnage, there are two outstanding questions to be answered, or at least posed. Why did Germany feel driven to this terrible expedient? Are the reasons mere excuses or do they add up to some sort of justification?

Right: H.M.S. *Majestic* on the way to the bottom after taking a direct hit from *U21*, 27 May 1915

5. WAR AGAINST COMMERCE

In November 1914 leaders of the German fleet approached Admiral von Pohl, Chief of the Naval Staff, with a proposal to turn U-boats loose against British and neutral shipping. Their case was well prepared and tightly reasoned. International law stipulated very clearly what a nation at war could and could not do in order to impede the trade of its enemies. Certain goods were contraband, others were described as conditional contraband, and others free. Contraband (war materials pure and simple) was liable to seizure regardless of its destination; conditional contraband (aids to war-making like food, fuel, and money) could be seized only if it was bound for enemy ports, or ports in enemy hands; free goods (textiles, much industrial equipment, and a host of manufactured goods) could not be touched unless they were being used as a cover for prohibited goods. All this was explicit, and formed part of the Declaration of London of 1909 which had been accepted by all the leading maritime powers—except Great Britain. The British had initially signed the agreement but had withheld ratification after second thoughts. They had realized (so the German argument ran) that the terms of the agreement made it impossible for Britain to conduct warfare along traditional lines, her traditional lines. Specifically, the distinction between contraband and conditional contraband made it impossible for her to employ the Royal Navy in its time-honoured role: throttling the enemy's economy. With their infuriating blend of ingenuousness and cynicism, with that smug self-righteousness which everyone had come to associate with them, they had simply announced that the agreement as it stood was inimical to British interests.

Now that war had come they were indulging in just the sort of brigandage that the London Agreement had outlawed. They were stopping conditional contraband bound for neutral countries, which was of great concern because Germany needed to import food through Holland. On 2 October they had announced to the world that they felt it necessary to mine the eastern end of the English Channel, leaving only a narrow stretch near their own coast (where naturally ships would be subject to British inspection). Now, a month later, they had just declared the entire North Sea a war zone. They scattered mine fields at will, and warned that ships straying from prescribed routes did so at their own risk: if they did not run into a mine they would surely encounter a British warship.

How was Germany to meet these flagrant breaches of international law? Their protests and the protests of neutrals were falling on deaf ears. The British intended to win the war by this painless method, painless for them that is, and there was not a ghost of a chance that they would relent under moral pressure. They must be answered with brute force. Either they must be forced to lift the blockade or they themselves must be blockaded, preferably both. But how? It would be suicidal

Admiral von Pohl, Chief of the German Naval Staff and firm advocate of a U-boat campaign against Allied commerce

Previous pages: Victims of U-boat raiders, the British *Glasgow* and the American *Illinois* (inset)

for the German fleet to contest the matter in a full-scale action. The British assumed, correctly, that German cruisers presented little threat to their own shipping. There remained only the U-boat.

The submarine, however, was peculiarly ill-suited to a campaign against commerce. It could hardly arrest a neutral ship because it could not spare the necessary crew members to take command. Nor, except under unusually favourable circumstances, could a submarine sink an enemy merchantman since there was no room aboard for captives. If the encounter took place close to shore in fairly calm conditions the seamen could make off in lifeboats, but it was certainly against international law to set men adrift on the high seas. Finally, a submarine ran a considerable risk in approaching merchant vessels on the surface, even if there were no warships in the offing. She would risk fire from a concealed gun at point-blank range or, equally fatal, she could be rammed. These disadvantages were so obvious that before the war the Germans had never thought of employing U-boats against British shipping. But they had not anticipated such lawlessness on the part of their enemy, and under these desperate circumstances the U-boat should be viewed in a new light. All the above disadvantages would vanish instantly if the U-boat ignored international law, in other words if merchant vessels were attacked without warning and without regard for the fate of their crews.

So the case was made. Germany should declare the waters around the British Isles blockaded. Any ship of any nation found within those waters should summarily be destroyed, and the justification for this ruthless, indeed illegal policy should be that Britain herself had sown the seeds of lawlessness and must therefore reap a bitter harvest. What about world opinion, or at least the opinion of neutrals and particularly the United States? The British were getting away with flouting world opinion and Germany could do the same. But were the British sinking neutral ships and leaving civilians to drown? Would the rest of the world, and again the Americans in particular, consider the policies equally culpable? They would unless they were blinded by ignorance or steeped in British hypocrisy. This was total war and the British had demonstrated that the old rules no longer applied. Their undisguised aim was to keep food out of Germany and thereby literally starve a civilian population into submission. Furthermore by mining international waters they were putting the lives of neutral civilians in jeopardy. Neutrals could avoid this peril only by staying clear of the restricted areas. They could avoid the U-boat peril in the same way. Only a fool or a knave could argue that there was a moral difference.

Argument there was, although not much of it connected with

ethics. Broadly speaking the German military and naval commands were for the campaign, and they enjoyed popular support. The government was against it and the Kaiser had grave reservations. It boiled down to the question of whether or not Germany could get away with it, whether the military advantages outweighed the political risk. If the neutrals contented themselves with protests and obeyed the restrictions—as they were obeying the British restrictions—then it would be a brilliant stroke, and one that would shorten the war. Then again, if the campaign was dramatically successful Britain would have to call off her blockade to get it stopped, in which case Germany would oblige, and the neutrals would be better off all round. On the other hand if the neutrals reacted violently and determined to help Britain at all costs, which meant if the Americans came into the war, it could be disastrous. It was a terrible gamble and the Germans knew it. As the war dragged on with that early victory steadily receding from sight, as the noose slowly tightened around German commerce, what had been a gamble started to seem a military necessity. On 4 February 1915 the waters round Great Britain and Ireland, including the English Channel, were declared a war zone. All British shipping would be sunk on sight and the safety of neutrals could not be guaranteed because of the difficulty of identifying flags at a distance, and also because of the unscrupulous British practice of running up neutral flags when the occasion demanded.

The Germans had not long to wait for neutral reaction, and in the face of American threats they hastily assured everybody that the greatest precautions would be taken to avoid sinking neutral ships. The naval men were bitterly disappointed with such a watered-down version of their original suggestion, but it was the best they could get. Thus began the first phase of the U-boat campaign, the so-called 'restricted' phase.

After all this debate, soul searching, and bluster, the events themselves proved a disappointing anti-climax. U-boats began taking a fairly regular toll, including a few neutral ships, but nothing like the tonnage needed to squeeze the enemy seriously. The neutrals were neither scared off (why would they be when the Germans were so painfully worried about sinking them?) nor did they show any signs of coming into the war. The British leapt at the chance to tighten their blockade, further abrogating the rights of neutrals with the usual excuses about warding off the murderous Hun. It is galling to find that a make-or-break policy neither makes nor breaks.

On the morning of 7 May *U20*, under Lieutenant-Commander Walther Schweiger, was starting for home after spending several days patrolling off the south coast of Ireland. As patrols at that stage went it had been successful but not spectacular: two steamers and one sailing vessel had been

The event that brought home the appalling consequences of submarine warfare: the sinking of the Cunard liner *Lusitania* on 7 May 1915. The Germans argued that their warning prominently displayed in American newspapers before the sailing exonerated them. The lethal blow is illustrated on the right and its effect below. The latter picture originally bore the caption 'Germany's "grand coup" in crime'

← Dotted line → represents approximate height of water & debris thrown up by the explosion

Approximate size of vast hole caused by Torpedo.

Torpedo

← Area affected (Rivets started Etc) →

PROMENADE DECK

SHELTER DECK

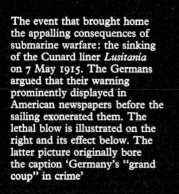

NOTICE.

Travellers intending to embark on Atlantic voyage are reminded that a state of war exists between Germany and her Allies and Great Britain and her Allies; that the zone of war includes the waters adjacent to the British Isles; that in accordance with the formal notice given by the Imperial German Government vessels flying the flag of Great Britain or any of her Allies are liable to destruction in those waters, and that travellers sailing in the war zone on ships of Great Britain or her Allies do so at their own risk.

Imperial German Embassy, Washington, D.C., April 22, 1915.

REMEMBER THE LUSITANIA!

One mother lost all her three young children, one six years, one aged four, and the third a babe in arms, six months old. She herself lives, and held up the three of them in the water, all the time shrieking for help. When rescued by a boat party the two eldest were dead. Their room was required on the boat, and the mother was brave enough to realise it. "Give them to me," she cried. "Give them to me, my bonnie wee things. I will bury them. They are mine to bury as they were mine to keep."

With her hair streaming down her back and her form shaking with sorrow, she took hold of each little one from the rescuers and reverently placed it into the water again, and the people in the boat wept with her as she murmured a little sobbing prayer to the great God above.

But her cup of sorrow was not yet completed. For just as they were landing, her third and only child died in her arms.

BERLIN, MAY 8.

Hundreds of *telegrams* have been sent to Admiral von Tirpitz congratulating him.

* * *

ARTICLE IN COLOGNE GAZETTE.

The news will be received by the German people with unanimous satisfaction, since it proves to England and the whole world that Germany is quite in earnest in regard to her submarine warfare.

* * *

ARTICLE IN KOLNISCHE VOLKSZEITUNG.

With joyful pride we contemplate the latest deed of our Navy and it will not be the last.

* * *

NEW YORK, MAY 8.

Riotous scenes of jubilation took place last evening amongst Germans in the German clubs and restaurants. Many Germans got drunk as the result of toasting "Der Tag."

ENLIST TO-DAY.

Nearly 1,200 died in the *Lusitania* disaster. Above: Mass burial of victims in Ireland. Left: The reaction in Britain—outrage and a ferocious propaganda campaign. Below: The reaction in Germany—a privately-struck medal showing Cunard as the death dealer

accounted for. Now, low on fuel and with only three torpedoes left, *U20* was making west from Waterford, taking the long way around in order to avoid the congested Irish Sea. Off the Old Head of Kinsale at 1.20 p.m., Schweiger saw a very large steamer sailing east, but on a course that would not bring her within torpedo range. At 1.40 the steamer changed direction and moved closer. At 2.09 *U20* fired at a range of 800 yards and caught the *Lusitania* squarely amidships. Moments later there was a second terrific explosion and within twenty minutes the great liner was gone.

The reaction was electrifying. Nearly 1,200 lives were lost, more than a hundred of them American. Protests flooded in as the reports came through, and they were not just British and American but world wide. It was a monstrous crime and it seemed to verify reams of British propaganda about German barbarism. The Germans reacted to this onslaught with a strange blend of wily cynicism and crass stupidity. They pointed out that the German ambassador to the United States had gone to the trouble of publishing a warning to those intending to embark on the *Lusitania*, several days before the sailing. The warning had been foolishly ignored. As for the mysterious second explosion, it had not been caused by a second torpedo but by vast quantities of ammunition that were being transported to Liverpool. This was neither convincing nor true, and as if Germany's reputation needed further marring the jubilation with which her leaders and populace hailed this 'triumph' was unrestrained. Schweiger was much fêted and a medal struck to commemorate the deed.

Leaving aside the moral question, the sinking of the *Lusitania* was a very grave error of judgement by the navy as it threw the U-boat campaign right back into the political arena. For nearly two years it remained there, to the bitter consternation of those who realized that Germany held in her hand only this one high card, and that it was probably the ace of trumps. The land war was not going according to the prearranged pattern. Millions strong, the armies of Europe were slugging it out on two fronts. The slaughter was dreadful, unprecedented, and there seemed no end to it. Yet end it must unless Germany somehow managed to break the deadlock, because she could not withstand indefinitely the remorseless blockade. It was weakening Germany terribly; it would cripple and destroy her.

Through the rest of 1915 and all 1916 the U-boat commanders fought with either one or both hands tied behind their backs. In the wake of the *Lusitania* uproar they were instructed to leave large passenger ships alone, although they began taking an increasing toll of merchant shipping. Then in August 1915 *U24* torpedoed and sank the small White Star liner *Arabic*, and under renewed protest the German government promised to attack passenger ships only after ensuring the safety of those on board. Under these handicaps the campaign in home waters ground to a halt in September, and while smaller submarines carried on with their mine-laying activities in the Channel, the main thrust against commerce turned to the Mediterranean. By the beginning of 1916 the political situation was less fraught (the Americans were complaining bitterly about the high-handed way the British were administering their blockade) and U-boats moved to the attack again, under hazy restrictions. Then in March the French cross-channel packet *Sussex* was torpedoed and the victims included a number of Americans. President Wilson threatened to break off diplomatic relations and the Germans backed down again: they promised to obey international law, which of course entirely drew the teeth from any U-boat campaign. And so it went on.

In October, U-boats again appeared in home waters, still more or less restricted in their operations, but now the policy began to bite hard because there were many more U-boats in service than there had been in 1915. They were sinking a far greater tonnage than Britain and her allies could replace, yet even on the most optimistic calculations the British were a long way from collapse. This was not the knockout blow the naval men had promised, but then it was not the fight they had asked for. By the beginning of 1917 pressures on the German government became intolerable. Germany would lose the war unless she cast off irresolution and attacked her enemies with every weapon at her disposal. On 9 January the Kaiser ordered unrestricted submarine warfare from 1 February.

During these two years the British had viewed the attack on their shipping with mounting concern, and by the autumn of 1916 with barely-concealed alarm. It was little use to command the seas when you could not even protect your own shipping in home waters, yet the idea that the submarine might be used in a *guerre de course* was not taken seriously until it happened. Before the war there had been a few ominous predictions that

U24, which caused another furore by sinking the liner *Arabic* in August 1915

The Germans bowed to the wave of protest following the *Arabic* incident, and announced that passenger ships would be attacked—if at all—only after the passengers were safe. Then in March 1916 the packet *Sussex* was torpedoed. Above: An American cartoon showing how a harmless paddle-steamer becomes a warship through a German periscope. Right: Another American cartoon showing the American eagle about to strike back at a demented Kaiser and ghoulish German ambassador to Washington (Bernstorf)

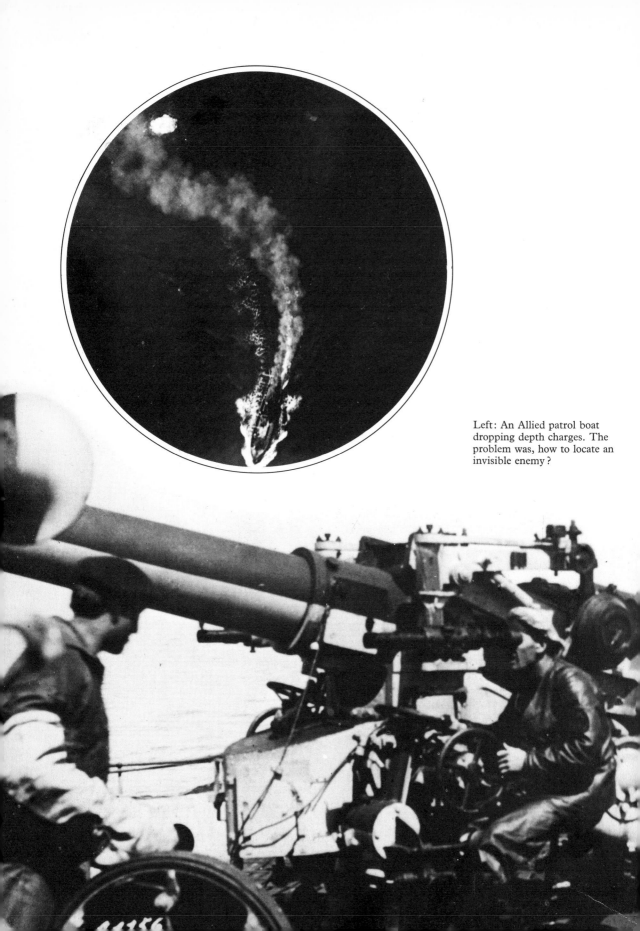

Left: An Allied patrol boat dropping depth charges. The problem was, how to locate an invisible enemy?

Britain's enemies might behave in this barbarous way but these warnings were discounted. The First Lord of the Admiralty, Winston Churchill, stated the general view when he expressed total disbelief that 'this would ever be done by a civilized power'. Now that it was being done it was of paramount importance to devise methods of defence, since even with artificial handicaps the U-boats were taking an unacceptable toll.

In this the British were singularly unsuccessful. Whereas capital ships managed to keep submarines more or less at bay either by staying in well-protected harbours or by moving at speed, ringed by escort destroyers, merchant ships must venture out and they were comparatively slow moving. They could ram an attacking submarine but it would be a careless submarine commander who allowed himself to be caught in that way. They could be armed, and in increasing numbers they were, but this was only a defence against a submarine attacking on the surface. So too were the Q-ships, decoys concealing heavy guns. Against the submerged U-boat there was no defence at all, at least in the early stages of the war. Eventually the hydrophone and depth-charge were developed: the hydrophone was an acoustic device that might locate a submerged submarine in very quiet conditions; the depth-charge was ahead of its time because its effective use demanded some better means of locating the quarry than that provided by the hydrophone. U-boats did occasionally come to grief on mines but not in significant numbers. One submarine could stalk another, but again it was pretty much a hit and miss affair.

While U-boats operated under the various restrictions imposed on them they were inclined to attack on the surface, since only in that way could they give warning or even be very sure who it was they were attacking. Working on the surface with a heavy gun had its advantages and disadvantages. It meant

Below: U-boat gunners. The great disadvantage of the gun as opposed to the torpedo was that the U-boat was more vulnerable to counter-attack

that small ships not worth a torpedo could still be sunk but of course it greatly increased the quarry's chances of escape and it meant that the U-boat was exposed to counter-attack. Over these two years there were many more surface attacks than there would have been had the U-boats operated with a free hand, and consequently their losses were much higher than necessary. When the terrible onslaught hit them in 1917 the British would find that their defensive measures counted for little, that their navy was powerless to defend them and bereft of ideas as to how they might defend themselves.

In the closing months of 1916 and January 1917 the losses to British and Allied shipping hovered around the appalling total of 300,000 tons per month, roughly double what it had been the previous summer. In February 1917, 469,000 tons of British, Allied, and neutral shipping perished. In March the total passed half a million tons. In April it skyrocketed to over 850,000 tons. The German government had agreed to the unrestricted campaign after being persuaded by the naval staff that destroying 600,000 tons per month would force Britain to her knees within six months, and the campaign was now exceeding all expectations. It did not matter that the United States had finally been driven into the war against Germany because the war would be over before the Americans arrived.

Despite America's entry into the war, April 1917 was one of the darkest moments in British history. Over 350 ships were sunk, one out of four making the outward journey never returned, and neutral shipping was finally being scared off. More than a hundred U-boats were in service and their numbers were increasing rapidly, more rapidly than they were being destroyed. It was freely admitted by the Admiralty that if things continued this way the war would be lost. When pressed for a solution the First Lord of the Admiralty, the distinguished Admiral Lord Jellicoe, replied that he had none except to try harder. What about the one defensive method still untried, the convoy system? It would not work for any number of reasons—all of them specious.

At this point Lloyd George realized that the leading men in the Admiralty were in a kind of stupor. They knew that the country was facing immediate ruin, and that a terrible weight of responsibility lay with them. They had no idea how to cope with the peril and they either could not or would not admit that where they had failed others might succeed. They were standing on the bridge with great dignity while the nation's ship sank beneath them. Lloyd George, who was not a good loser, pleaded, bullied, cajoled, and finally won grudging support for the convoy system. In May losses dropped to just below the March figures, but in June they topped 600,000 tons, and again in July.

According to German estimates that should have been enough. The U-boats had done what they said they would do

Above: American troopships bound for Europe in convoy, guarded by destroyers. It was by adopting the convoy system for merchant as well as troop and capital ships that the Allies finally took the measure of the U-boat

Previous pages: A rendezvous between two deadly war machines that came of age during the First World War. The German seaplane brings operational instructions to the U-boat

and more, yet for some reason Britain had not capitulated. The answer was to step up the pressure, and a crash building programme was launched. What they did not grasp was that the tide was turning against the U-boat. Britain had scraped through the crisis by a combination of good luck and good management. After wavering in the early months, the neutrals had resumed almost normal shipping; the Americans had sent over a great many destroyers immediately on entering the war, which ensured convoys of reasonable protection; perhaps most important, the British authorities had displayed far greater skill in managing a depleted economy than the Germans imagined possible. The worst was past and as the convoy system got into its stride the losses began to drop and the U-boat casualties began to rise inexorably.

The idea of grouping merchant ships together and shepherding them across dangerous waters under the protection of escort vessels is a very old one, and it must be the nub of any rational attempt to ward off a serious assault on sea communications. The convoy system has two outstanding virtues. First, it exposes the raider to counter-attack. Admittedly the U-boats were less vulnerable on this score than surface ships would have been because of the near impossibility of locating them before they struck. But convoy escorts could at least deny U-boats the luxury of attacking on the surface in broad daylight. Moreover when a U-boat did attack a convoy it could not pick off ships at leisure, one after the other. The escorts would see the torpedo tracks and race along them dropping depth-charges. These counter-attacks achieved only modest successes in terms of U-boats destroyed but they did make life a great deal more hazardous for the marauders. If one is incapable of dealing harshly with commerce raiders it is well at least to inconvenience them.

The second argument in favour of convoys is even more telling. A flotilla of twenty-five ships is more conspicuous than one ship alone—but only marginally. It is nothing like twenty-five times as conspicuous. What this means is that even without armed escorts, ships are less at risk if they sail in groups. It must be remembered that shipping lanes are not like highways. The Atlantic Ocean is vast, and U-boats had no hope of forming even a loose net across the Western Approaches to the British Isles. A U-boat might certainly wreak havoc with a convoy but first it had to find one, and it was this comparative elusiveness of ships in convoy that proved their greatest salvation.

This does not mean that the U-boat campaign was defeated in the summer of 1917. It continued right to the final stages of the war, to the autumn of 1918, and in a sense it was never really defeated, it merely failed. It failed in its self-appointed task of winning the war single-handed, but it was a very near thing. In the most compelling way the submarine had staked its position among the weapons of war.

6. BETWEEN THE WARS

The British drew no comforting conclusions from their salvation. They had not in the end succumbed to the U-boat campaign but it had been a brush with death. The experience confirmed all those dire warnings about the threat to Britain of underwater gunboats, from St Vincent onwards, and confirmed them with a vengeance. It was of paramount concern that the British Isles never again be imperilled in this way. The elementary first step was to obliterate the entire German submarine fleet, and this was accomplished with dispatch. By the terms of the Naval Armistice 176 serviceable U-boats were surrendered to the Allies, and with a few exceptions they went straight to the bottom. More than 200 unserviceable or unfinished U-boats were destroyed where they lay. To clinch the matter, the Treaty of Versailles stipulated that Germany could keep, build, or buy no submarines.

While this left the Royal Navy in possession of the largest and most advanced submarine fleet in the world, things were not allowed to rest there. When the five major naval powers (Britain, France, the United States, Italy, and Japan) met at Washington in 1921 Britain pressed for a total ban on submarines. The case was argued on moral grounds, but it was a tacit admission that Britain had more to fear from submarines than anyone else, which was abundantly evident to all. The motion found no support, and the Treaty of Washington placed no restrictions whatever on submarine construction, although only the French were unwilling to pledge themselves never to engage in the sort of commerce-raiding that had been so recently witnessed.

Throughout the inter-war years Britain continued to press for abolition of the submarine and failing that for restrictions.

Previous pages: German submariners take final leave of their U-boat after the fleet has been interned

Right: The German Fleet interned at Scapa Flow was scuttled by the Germans on 21 June 1919. A salvage party boards a German destroyer

Below: U-boats interned at Harwich on 24 November 1918, two weeks after the Armistice

Yet it would have been folly to anticipate success in such a campaign. Should it prove impossible to outlaw the weapon then it would be advisable both to possess the best and to develop some effective means of self-protection for surface vessels. To the former end, work on advanced submarines that had been in progress when the Armistice came was continued. Three-quarters of the surviving boats were scrapped, leaving under fifty still in commission. These included many of the reliable E types, and their successors, the Gs, Js, and Ls, as well as the experimental steam-powered Ks. The K-boat was an attempt to provide a fleet submarine, but while the surface performance was impressive and the diving time much reduced from that of previous steam-powered submarines, K-boats achieved nothing during the war. The British also possessed two other quite revolutionary submarines, although neither was completed in time to see action. The 'monitor' submarines, or M-boats, were armed with a twelve-inch gun, which had a much greater range than any torpedo but did not have the advantage of being fired from concealment. The R-boats were at the other end of the spectrum: designed for attacking other submarines, they were small, very fast under water, and equipped with six bow torpedo tubes. The idea of positioning all the torpedo tubes in the bow rather than distributing them among the bow, the beams, and the stern, was carried over into succeeding classes of patrol submarines and marked a significant advance. So too did increasing the tube size from 18 to 21 inches, which became standard on patrol submarines.

Despite this steady progress, which kept British submarines in the lead technically if not numerically, it was in the closely related field of anti-submarine development that Britain made the more gratifying breakthrough. The asdic (the name comes from the initial letters of the wartime Allied Submarine Detection Investigation Committee) was a device for locating submerged submarines, and it was no mere listening device like the hydrophone. Fitted to the bottom of a destroyer and moved slowly through a wide arc, the asdic could transmit and receive signals. When the sound waves struck a submarine they bounced back, and the echoing 'ping' was picked up by the receiver. The elapsed time between sending out the signal and hearing the answering 'ping' told the asdic operator how far away the submarine was. Then, checking the 'fix' repeatedly, the destroyer could close in for a depth-charge attack. Whether or not asdic would tilt the scales decisively against the submarine in any future war was an open question, but that it would go some way towards removing the submarine's greatest asset, its cloak of invisibility, was certain.

By the time the five naval powers assembled for the London Conference of 1931 the balance of submarine strength had changed significantly. Though they were not represented at the

British experimental submarines. Top: *K3*, the first of the K class, was completed during the First World War but did not see action. These large fleet submarines were very fast (24 knots) but their steam engines made it impossible for them to dive quickly. Above: The monitor class submarine *M2*, which was converted to a mini aircraft carrier. She was lost in 1931 when the locking device on the hangar door failed. Right: *M1*, equipped with a 12-inch gun in place of torpedoes

Conference, the Russians had begun a very large construction programme in 1928. At the close of the inter-war period they had more submarines than anyone else, but they were almost all designed for coastal defence. The Americans, the French, and the Japanese all had more submarines in commission than the British, who again pressed for abolition. Again they failed, although it was agreed that the British tonnage (which was only slightly less than the American and French) would not be exceeded. This, combined with faith in the 'secret' asdic, allowed the British to view the submarine menace with greater equanimity. It was still a weapon that would best be done away with but it was no longer considered a threat of scarifying proportions. Events would show this to be a wild miscalculation, but in 1931 it seemed plausible, and like a great many other comforting assumptions of the early 1930s it lingered on long after it had become a dangerous delusion.

Hitler swept to power in early 1933, and by the next year the Germans were secretly building U-boats. In March 1935 the Nazi dictator repudiated the Treaty of Versailles and the sorry drama of appeasement began to unfold. A month later the British, recognizing the fact that Hitler was building a navy and that there was nothing short of force that could prevent him from doing so, negotiated the Anglo-German Naval Agreement. This

R27 being launched in September 1918. Like the Ks and Ms, the Rs came into service too late to see action. They were designed for attacking enemy submarines and were small, speedy, and heavily armed

permitted Germany to build up a navy provided that it did not exceed 35 per cent of the tonnage of the British navy. The single exception to this 35 per cent limit was the U-boat arm which could reach 45 per cent, and under loosely-defined 'extra-ordinary' circumstances complete parity with British submarines. At the same time Hitler gave support to the old stringent rules about commerce-raiding, which were restated in the London Submarine Agreement of 1936.

Captain Karl Doenitz, who had served as a submariner during the First World War, was put in charge of the new U-boat service. This was an inspired choice, and had Hitler and the naval head Admiral Raeder extended their confidence in Doenitz's ability to a belief in his strategical foresight then the Second World War might have taken a very different course. For Doenitz, unlike his superiors, quickly came to the conclusion that a general European war was coming in the near future, that Britain would inevitably be ranged against Germany, and that the development of a powerful U-boat fleet should receive top priority. It seemed to him self-evident that the U-boat would again be involved in a war to the death with British commerce. Moreover he drew startlingly original—and correct—conclusions about the failure of the U-boat campaign of 1917–18. The campaign would have succeeded, he argued, if there had been more U-boats and if they had been deployed differently. The belated adoption of the convoy system had thwarted the U-boat only because U-boat tactics had not been altered to cope with the changed situation. The answer to the convoy was the 'wolf-pack', a concentration of U-boats working as a team. Small, fast, and highly manoeuvrable U-boats would be ideally suited—and Doenitz wanted 300 of them as quickly as they could be built.

He was countered at every turn. Hitler and Raeder were convinced that full-scale war would not come for many years if it came at all, and that Britain would not fight in any case unless her trading links with the rest of the world were threatened. Hitler was genuinely prepared to let Britain rule the waves—and why not? He wanted nothing from Britain but to be left alone, and the way to ensure this was to appeal to British self-interest. The British disliked ructions on the Continent but they *fought* to protect their purse. Germany needed a navy (and U-boats were a natural part of the navy) but nothing like the great fleet of twenty-five years before which had provoked Britain and then been unable to defeat her. The naval building programme therefore envisaged a moderately powerful fleet completed by 1948, and even then with considerably fewer U-boats than Doenitz was agitating for immediately.

At the same time Doenitz failed to convince his superiors that large U-cruisers were a comparative waste of time. The Type VII U-boat, 500 tons and equipped with five torpedo tubes, was perfectly suited to convoy attacks in the Western Approaches to the British Isles or even in mid-Atlantic, and Doenitz urged that maximum effort be devoted to producing this small wolf-pack U-boat. While he received a considerable number of them, priority was still given to long-range U-cruisers, armed with a heavy gun and therefore capable of operating in compliance with international law. At the same time a great many very small U-boats were built, of 250 tons displacement and suitable for use only in the North Sea. So it was that Germany entered the Second World War with a mixed bag of fifty-seven submarines rather than 300 specially-designed convoy raiders.

War in September 1939 caught not only the U-boat arm but the entire German navy in a state of woeful unpreparedness. The British navy was not what it had been in 1914 but its relative strength was very much greater. Against fourteen capital ships and seven aircraft carriers the Germans could oppose only two battle cruisers and three pocket battleships. The Germans realized that naval engagement in the classical sense was therefore completely out of the question, and that Germany could make her presence felt at sea only by a direct attack on commerce, both with surface ships and U-boats. In one sense this was an advantage because it freed naval minds from any cant about cutting the British fleet down to manageable size while protecting the German fleet. The target was British commerce and there was no time wasted in debating this.

Above: *U565*, one of the new VIIC class which came into service early in the Second World War. Right: *U2*, one of the IIA class of coastal submarines developed in the inter-war years

Left: Karl Doenitz, the man who assumed command of the new U-boat service in 1935. He wanted 300 U-boats immediately; fortunately for the future Allies he did not get them, and had only one-fifth that number by 1939

7.THE BATTLE OF THE ATLANTIC

On 3 September 1939 Great Britain declared war on Germany, and on the same day *U30* torpedoed and sank the passenger ship *Athenia,* bound for the United States. Hitler had issued strict orders that U-boat warfare be conducted legally and the attack on the *Athenia* was without doubt a blunder on the part of *U30*'s commander. The reactions were predictable. The British called it a crime, which it certainly was, and assumed that they were once again to suffer an unrestricted U-boat campaign, this time at the hands of an enemy so unscrupulous that he had not even bothered to announce his intentions. The Germans compounded their error with evasion, denials, and ludicrous counter-charges. In fact, Hitler was furious at being embarrassed and still anxious to avoid an armed clash with Britain and France, who he fondly believed might leave the war before they became actively committed—so long as they were allowed to make a graceful exit. He tightened up the restrictions on U-boat operations even further, and the results merely confirmed what was known from the First World War: submarines make little impression on commerce unless they are employed with a ruthless disregard for the accepted rules of warfare. As the autumn of 1939 dragged

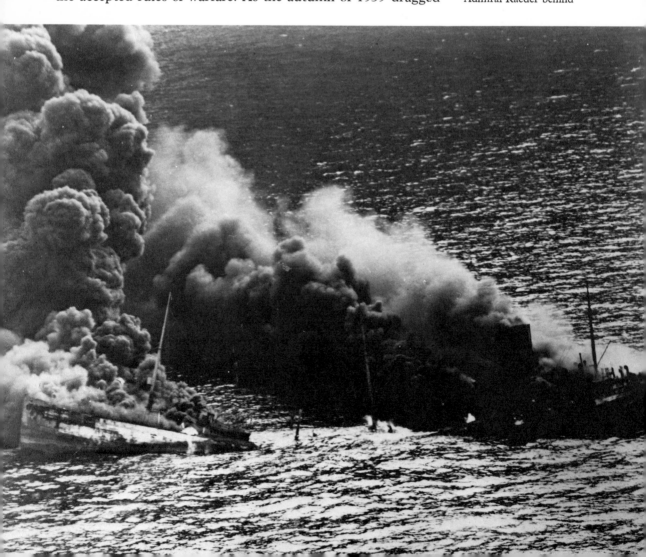

on without peace signals from Britain and France the mood hardened, and one after another the restrictions came off. At this stage of the war, however, it was not against merchant shipping that U-boats scored their most noteworthy successes.

On 14 September the British aircraft carrier *Ark Royal* was attacked unsuccessfully but on the 17th another carrier, the *Courageous*, was sunk with the loss of over 500 men. A month later Lieutenant-Commander Gunther Prien in *U47* pulled off one of the most spectacular exploits of the war. He stole into Scapa Flow and put two torpedoes into the battleship *Royal Oak*, which sank in minutes with heavy loss of life. *U47* escaped, and while her great triumph owed much to the ineptness of the British defences it greatly enhanced the U-boat's prestige. Such an opportunity would not present itself again, but it was hardly the area in which Doenitz expected to deliver his enemy a mortal blow. U-boat construction was stepped up; a disturbing but not critical number of merchant ships were sunk; the 'phoney war' dragged on.

In the spring of 1940 the Nazi sledgehammer struck western Europe and shattered it to bits. In April Denmark was occupied and Norway invaded. In May Holland, Belgium, and Luxembourg surrendered. On the 27th of that month British forces began their memorable escape from Dunkirk. June brought Italy's 'stab in the back' and the capitulation of France. On 1 July the Channel Islands were in enemy hands. It was Nazi Germany's 'finest hour'.

Now, at this terrible ebb in Britain's fortunes, the U-boat campaign was getting into its stride. Although Churchill did not coin the phrase until the next year this was the beginning of the Battle of the Atlantic. In June nearly 300,000 tons of shipping were sunk. The figure dropped by a third in July, but was up again in August and September. In October it totalled 352,000 tons. These figures may seem low when compared with those of the dark days of 1917 but the losses far exceeded replacements. Moreover, this was no desperate attempt by an exhausted combatant to stave off defeat. Germany was triumphant on land, and while during this period she failed to master the skies over England, her leaders and people had every reason to suppose that time was on their side. These successes were being achieved by a U-boat arm that was still in its infancy. Simple arithmetic showed what Britain could expect when U-boats put to sea in strength. Finally, the British this time did not have the obvious solution at hand, waiting only to be tried. They had instituted a convoy system as soon as war broke out.

This opening phase of the Battle of the Atlantic was cheerfully described by German submariners as 'the happy time', and so it was, for them. But why were they finding so little difficulty in confronting asdic and the escorted convoy? In the first place asdic was nothing like as formidable as the Germans had feared

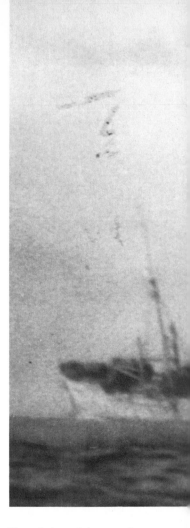

Two victims of the torpedo. Above: An ex-French ship in German service, photographed through the periscope of an American submarine at the moment of impact. Right: The last moments of an Allied freighter prey to a U-boat

and the British had confidently expected. It was very easy to mistake other underwater objects for submarines, whales for instance, and even when a U-boat was correctly identified asdic could provide only a rough guide as to its depth, which meant that depth-charges might well be dropped in the right place only to explode harmlessly. Asdic suffered from another, even greater liability: it was ill-suited to picking up small objects on the surface. For some reason the British confidently assumed that U-boats would for the most part attack from a submerged position during the daytime. They were surprised to find Doenitz employing the tactics developed in 1918 when the heavy concentration of armed escorts made daylight attacks on convoys risky, even for a submerged U-boat. The answer was to attack on the surface at night. U-boats were faster on the surface than the vast majority of merchant ships and with their low silhouette they were very difficult to see. They could dodge the escorts (undetected by asdic) and move right into the heart of the convoy.

By the autumn of 1940 Doenitz was also beginning to try out his theory of mass attack by U-boats working in close co-operation, and despite the relatively few U-boats available the wolf-pack was living up to his predictions. The tactics were

The ubiquitous *U47* setting out for the high seas

simple and deadly effective. When a U-boat sighted a convoy
it radioed the Operations control, which Doenitz had set up in
France. Control immediately called in other U-boats in the
vicinity, while the first U-boat would be content with shadowing
the convoy until the others arrived. Then they would strike in
concert, their deployment governed by the situation as it
unfolded, and by instructions from control, which was able to
develop a comprehensive picture of the battle from the stream
of individual reports. At its best the operation was conducted
with the precision of a radio-controlled police raid.

The events of 18 and 19 October 1940 stand as a chilling
reminder of the U-boat's early ascendency over the convoy. The
calamity that befell the convoys SC7 and HX79 on these nights,
the high point of 'the happy time', is unrepresentative in the
sense that it was particularly and memorably dreadful. It was
also the first time the wolf-pack went into operation, and being
unexpected the new tactics were especially successful. Yet the
disaster was not unparalleled and it brings into stark relief the
magnitude of the task facing the Allies as they struggled for
three years to master the threat.

SC7 comprised thirty-five ships making the eastward crossing
from Sydney, Cape Breton Island. Until it reached the Western
Approaches it was guarded by a single sloop, but at 21° 30′ west

it was joined by another sloop and a corvette. Thus escorted it made steady and uneventful progress through the night of 16 October, but it was unlucky enough to come within sight of *U48*. Six other U-boats raced to intercept the convoy but in the meantime the comander of *U48* decided to attack alone, and at 4 p.m. on the 17th he torpedoed and sank two of the freighters. *U48* then lost contact with the convoy, and while *U38* picked it up the following night her torpedoes did little damage. The wolves, however, were now closing in. As night fell on the 18th the work of destruction began. As the escorts dashed wildly about trying in vain to locate the intruders, torpedoes struck home with monotonous regularity, sending ship after ship to the bottom. The U-boat commanders set about their work systematically, like workers in an abattoir. All through the night explosions rocked the stricken convoy and when daylight finally brought the carnage to an end there were only fifteen ships afloat, two of them damaged. The remnants of the convoy were left in peace as the U-boats turned back out to sea where another convoy had been reported.

HX79, which consisted of forty-nine ships crossing from Halifax, Nova Scotia, was now entering the Western Approaches, two days behind SC7. It was very much more heavily guarded than the earlier convoy. On the 18th the two armed merchant ships that had accompanied HX79 across the Atlantic were joined by two destroyers, a minesweeper, four corvettes, and three trawlers. They were also joined by Prien in *U47*, although they did not know that. *U47* had no torpedoes left and was shadowing the convoy as all U-boats in the vicinity rushed to join her. By the evening of the 19th the pack was assembled and shortly after nine o'clock the attack began. The powerful escort availed HX79 nothing and twelve ships went down during the night. The U-boats emerged unscathed and, having used up their torpedoes, broke from the convoy and headed back to their base. From that point onwards the wolf pack was standard operational procedure; as more U-boats became available the patrols were extended; as the personnel gained experience so the techniques were refined and perfected.

Britain's troubles did not stem only from an over-reliance on asdic and the inability to foresee the tactics Doenitz would employ against convoys. At the root of the problem was a misconception of the true function of the armed convoy. The British thought of it as a purely defensive measure to protect merchant shipping. They could not see the reverse side of the coin, that the armed convoy was the only feasible means of waging *offensive* war against the U-boat. They persisted in the delusion that surface patrolling was the answer, and not only was this wrong but it meant that destroyers and other potential escort vessels were wasted in fruitless searches when they were badly needed for convoy work. It is difficult to understand why this

The Soviet submarine *K21* of the Northern Fleet, which claimed fourteen enemy ships in 1944

fundamental mistake was made since the logic of the situation is so clear. If U-boats are hunting for convoys there is no point in hunting for U-boats. The thing to do is ensure that every convoy is sufficiently well protected so that a U-boat attacks at its peril. This is true whether U-boats are working alone or in packs. If the latter then it simply means that defences must be much stronger, stronger even than they were for HX79, and very much more experienced. The outcome of the Battle of the Atlantic, of which this was only the first round, would depend on how quickly and how thoroughly this lesson was learned.

From November 1940 to January 1942 the struggle continued with neither side gaining the upper hand, although things were never as black for the Allies as they had been during 'the happy time'. The convoy system improved and eventually spread right across the ocean, in response to the ever-expanding U-boat sweeps. At the same time the Allies became more imaginative in their anti-submarine techniques. They made good use of intercepted U-boat messages and they began to fight back with radar-equipped aircraft. The losses to shipping were severe but not crippling, and had the situation not altered radically the Battle of the Atlantic might have settled into stalemate. On 11 December 1941 the United States declared war on Germany.

This formal declaration, whatever it might mean in the long run, was an immediate gift to the U-boat commanders. The fictional neutrality had long hampered their operations in the western Atlantic since Hitler was extremely loathe to provoke the Americans. Yet from September 1941 destroyers of the U.S. navy were escorting outward-bound convoys, and were instructed to attack U-boats. This amounted to undeclared war, and on 29 October the destroyer *Reuben James* was sunk during a convoy battle. Even here the U-boat was in a defensive posture—scarcely its chosen role. If the Americans thought that open warfare would make little difference to the existing state of affairs then they made a grave mistake.

Doenitz promptly dispatched the five U-boats immediately available to the east coast of the United States. They came across an incredible scene. The heaviest concentration of shipping in the world was steaming unconcerned up and down the seaboard. There were no convoys and no escorts. The ships were not blacked-out at night and as an added bonus they were perfectly silhouetted by the glare of lights from towns and cities dotted along the coast. The Americans, it seemed, had learned nothing from the British experience of two world wars. The U-boats had a field-day. They moved boldly into the shipping lanes at nightfall and proceeded to shoot down their targets like so many sitting ducks. For six months the slaughter ran freely, limited only by the number of U-boats available. Losses were exceeding half a million tons a month before the Americans began gathering their coastal shipping into convoys. They

neglected, however, to extend this policy to the Caribbean. To their consternation (and surprise!) the U-boats swarmed into these unprotected waters and continued their sport. The June sinking totalled 752,000 tons, the highest since April 1917. In July, convoys were hastily thrown together everywhere, and the contest swung back into mid-ocean. Here in a furious crescendo the Battle of the Atlantic was won and lost.

Doenitz was fully aware that the salad days were gone forever. He knew that he faced convoys at every turn and he knew that U-boat tactics were not keeping pace with the improved defences and very probably could not. He must be prepared to withstand much higher casualties in a trial of strength on the high seas. The question was whether the convoys or the wolf-packs would break first. The battleground was not of Doenitz's choosing but it was the only one where he stood a chance. Convoys enjoyed air support far out into the Atlantic on each side and these aeroplanes now possessed vastly improved radar sets which put surfaced U-boats in great danger, even in bad weather. However, there was a gap of about 500 miles where the air support could not reach, and this is where Doenitz made his stand. From August 1942 to April 1943 the battle raged back and forth, with both sides taking appalling losses. Despite terrible punishment the U-boats more than ever held their own and their numbers slowly increased. The Allies tried desperately to close the gap, throwing more and longer-range aeroplanes—and finally aircraft carriers—into the fray. In March the U-boats ripped apart convoy after convoy and sank more than 600,000 tons. In April they reached out for victory and found it slipping from their grasp. In May their world fell apart. In a series of murderous actions forty-one U-boats perished and on the 24th of that month Doenitz signalled the retreat. The losses were insupportable—regardless of the amount of shipping sunk—and the Battle of the Atlantic was over. For the remainder of the war U-boat operations continued in a sporadic fashion but they never again threatened to cut Allied communications. In 1917 the U-boat had been stymied by the convoy. In 1943 it was very nearly massacred.

Twelve days before Doenitz recalled his U-boats from the North Atlantic the Axis powers suffered a disaster of the first magnitude in another theatre of war. On 12 May 1943 their remaining forces in North Africa, overwhelmed by land, sea, and air, surrendered on the shores of Tunisia. For the Allies it was the triumphant conclusion to three years of bitter fighting during which they had faced ruin more than once. For the British submarine service the Mediterranean campaign was the convincing victory that had been denied it in the Baltic and the Sea of Marmara during the First World War. Admittedly the laurels were shared, but without submarines there would have been none to share.

Left: Victory over a U-boat: the captain of a British destroyer approaches *U570* to accept her surrender

8.THE BATTLE OF THE MEDITERRANEAN

When France collapsed a few days after Mussolini threw in his lot with Hitler in June 1940, the British found themselves confronted in the Mediterranean with a situation unusual and abhorrent to them. Their Mediterranean fleet, based on Alexandria, could not hope to provide them with mastery of the sea. This was not in itself cause for despair because British forces in the Middle East could, with inconvenience, be supplied by way of the long Cape route. It was imperative, however, to cut—or at least interrupt—communications between Italy and the Italian army in Libya. Later on it would be vital to prevent supplies of any sort from reaching Rommel's Afrika Korps, wherever it happened to be. In a curious reversal of the situation in the Atlantic, the British were forced to dispute waters in which they did not enjoy a naval superiority, with the aim of crippling an enemy who had no choice but to transport goods by sea and by predictable routes.

The war in the Mediterranean began in a minor key principally because the Italian navy showed little inclination to fight and the British, unable to maintain naval vessels at the near-defenceless Malta, were in no position to force an action. Whatever the failings of the Italian navy, Britain's neglect of Malta in the inter-war years was terrible folly and it cost her fighting men dearly. A strong air presence on this strategically-located island would have given the British matchless opportunities to shadow the Italian navy and to harass convoys. As it was, even the handful of British submarines were forced to flee to the safety of Alexandria. Fortunately for the British their stupid lack of foresight was equalled in the long run by their enemy's mystifying failure to understand that bombing Malta was no substitute for capturing it.

Despite the fact that carrier-based aircraft knocked out half the Italian fleet at Taranto in November, the strategic position altered little for the remainder of 1940. Although the British managed to strengthen and supply the garrison left behind at Malta they made a negligible impact on the Italian supplies crossing to Libya—and later to Greece. This particular phoney war came to an abrupt end when Hitler dispatched the crack Fliegerkorps X to Sicily. The British fleet, and the garrison at Malta, were quickly made aware of the awesome power of the dive-bomber, and the balance of power in the Mediterranean switched dramatically. In February the newly-formed Afrika Korps began arriving in Tripoli. In May the British were forced to evacuate Crete, with heavy loss to the British fleet. In the dark days of spring 1941 it was only British submarines that could provide any ray of light for the Allies.

The Malta Flotilla, comprising ten small submarines of the U class, had been built up gradually during the comparative lull of late 1940. In the crisis brought about by complete Axis air supremacy these submarines were the most effective Allied

Previous pages: British power in the Mediterranean was shaken by the loss of the aircraft carrier *Ark Royal*, torpedoed by *U81* on 13 November 1941

Top right: The British submarine base at Malta—the key to Allied success in the Mediterranean

Centre: The Italian cruiser *Muzio Attendolo* after being torpedoed by the British submarine *Unbroken*

Bottom: H.M.S. *Upshot*, one of the small band of U class submarines that played havoc with Italian supply lines to north Africa in early 1941

striking force, and during the opening months of 1941 they began hitting hard at the North African supply routes. Their crews were both expert and brave and the submarines deserved their confident, aggressive names—*Unbeaten, Upholder, Unique, Utmost, Upright,* and so on. Lieutenant-Commander Malcolm Wanklyn in *Upholder* was outstanding, and on the evening of 25 May the Italian Navy suffered a catastrophe at his hands. Just south of Messina Wanklyn spotted four heavily guarded troopships, and although *Upholder* had only two torpedoes left Wanklyn moved to the attack. Both torpedoes slammed into the *Conte Rosse* and *Upholder* weathered a barrage of depth-charges before slipping away—while the *Conte Rosse* sank with the loss of more than 1,200 troops. In August another troopship was sunk, this time by *Unique,* and then in September Wanklyn in *Upholder* struck again. In the early hours of the 18th *Unbeaten* spotted a troop convoy racing from Taranto to Tripoli. This convoy was anticipated and *Unbeaten* was patrolling in search of it, along with *Upright, Ursula,* and *Upholder.* The British 'wolf-pack' closed in on the three troopships and Wanklyn promptly sank the *Neptunia* and badly damaged the *Oceania.* While a third troopship escaped the onslaught Wanklyn submerged until daylight and then sank the *Oceania* with two more torpedoes.

Control of the central Mediterranean was now slipping away

Lieutenant-Commander Malcolm Wanklyn (bearded) receives congratulations on being awarded the Victoria Cross for his role in sinking the *Conte Rosse* (May 1941). Less than a year later Wanklyn and the crew of *Upholder* were killed in action

The slow death of H.M.S. *Ark Royal*. A skeleton crew stayed aboard in a vain attempt to save the carrier (top). She could not be brought back to even keel (note the frightening slope of the flight deck). In the bottom photograph a destroyer moves in to take off survivors. All but one were saved

Left: H.M.S. *Barham* explodes
after being torpedoed by *U331*,
25 November 1941. More than
800 men died

Below: An Italian 'chariot', the
two-man torpedo which
knocked the battleships
Valiant and *Queen Elizabeth* out
of action in December 1941

Right: The damage to
H.M.S. *Valiant*

from the Axis. In June Hitler had recalled most of his aircraft for the assault on Russia, and Malta was assuming for the Allies the role it should never have been denied. Malta-based bombers slashed at Rommel's lifeline, and by November the combined assault by aircraft, submarines, and surface raiders was accounting for three out of four Axis supply ships. Despite Hitler's obsession with the Russian campaign this state of affairs could not be ignored. Refusing to pull aircraft back from the Russian front Hitler instead prized twenty U-boats from Raeder, and by November ten of them were in the Mediterranean. Results were not long in coming: on 13 November the carrier *Ark Royal* was sunk by *U81*; on the 25th the battleship *Barham* was torpedoed by *U331* and blew up, with the loss of 868 lives.

It was not only at the hands of German U-boats that British warships suffered during this period. On the night of 18 December six Italian frogmen performed an astounding feat. They emerged from the submarine *Scire* astride three slow-moving torpedoes, two men on each, and stole undetected into Alexandria harbour. Detachable warheads were affixed to the hulls of the battleships *Valiant* and *Queen Elizabeth* and both were damaged seriously enough to put them out of action for several months, and with them the Eastern battle fleet. This spectacular 'chariot' raid in combination with the U-boat successes meant the temporary eclipse of the Mediterranean fleet, but it did not take any pressure off the Axis supply routes to North Africa. This was the crucial battle, and if Hitler seemed now and again to lose sight of this fact Rommel and Mussolini were unflagging in their efforts to remind him. On 2 December Hitler ordered Fliegerkorps II to Sicily and the bombardment of Malta began in earnest.

From January to May 1942 the Allied position became even worse than it had been a year earlier. Malta was nearly pulverized

Above: The submarine depot ship *Medway*, sunk by *U372* in June 1942—a crushing blow for the Allies

Below: The German *U35* holds an Allied freighter at her mercy in the Mediterranean

by airstrikes—more than 200 of them in April alone—and those surface warships not destroyed were evacuated. The submarine base was maintained until May, under the most hazardous conditions, but during this period it could make little impression on the Libyan convoys; so desperate was Malta's plight that submarines were pressed into service as supply ships. To put matters seemingly beyond hope *U372* torpedoed and sank the submarine depot ship *Medway* at the end of June, thereby paralyzing what remained of the Allied submarine campaign.

At this critical juncture, with Malta prostrate and Rommel sweeping all before him, the Germans committed a grievous error. They mistook impending victory for victory itself and recalled much of their air striking force to the Russian theatre. Simultaneously the Allies managed to re-establish a powerful air arm on Malta, and while the threat of starvation still hung over the island the crisis had passed. By the end of July submarines were back in strength and the Libyan convoys were again taking a fearful hammering. As his Panzer Army squared up with Montgomery's Eighth Army for the showdown at El Alamein Rommel faced crippling shortages. In the month of October, when the great battle began, he received less than half the gasoline sent him, and this fuel shortage was a major factor in the German disaster. As Rommel's shattered forces reeled westward before the victorious Eighth Army the Allied landings in North Africa were under way. It was, in Churchill's words, 'the end of the beginning'.

Three German and two Italian divisions poured into Tunisia in a misguided attempt to salvage something from the situation that was already lost, and for this they paid a terrible price. The influx of troops to Tunisia merely aggravated the supply problem and, as 1943 opened, the assault on Italian shipping became slaughter. By March the losses were approaching 50 per cent. In April they were even higher and by the end of that month nothing of any consequence was getting through. Hitler continued to rant about fighting on to the last man, but to a starving army the appeal of ritualistic suicide was remote. Defeat was total, and from that time forward the Mediterranean was open to Allied shipping. For neither side did submarine activity in the Mediterranean end with the war in North Africa, but for both it took on a more subdued character. Allied submarines stayed on to assist with the invasion of Sicily and to hunt down the remaining U-boats. For their part the U-boats continued to prowl these inhospitable waters until the last of them was sunk. So ended the first naval campaign in which submarines played a major role in victory, oddly enough on the side of that power which had suffered most painfully at their hands in both world wars. Meanwhile, on the other side of the globe, submarines were living up to the great expectations of Doenitz, although in circumstances he could hardly relish.

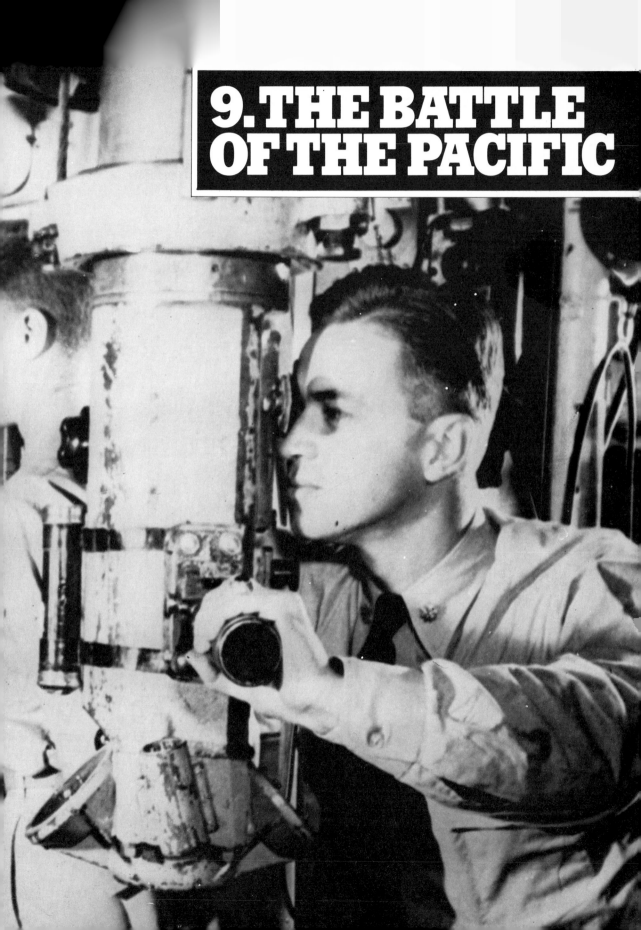

9. THE BATTLE OF THE PACIFIC

The Japanese sneak attack on Pearl Harbor was, whether it should have been or not, completely unexpected by the Americans. But if the nature of the assault and its target came as a surprise the war itself did not, and both the American and Japanese navies envisaged an important role for submarines in the conflict ahead. Moreover they were fairly equal in submarine strength and each planned to employ its submarines in the same way, for strikes against enemy warships. The use of submarines in war was a new departure for both sides and events would show that neither began with a clear vision of what to expect from it. The Japanese fatally overestimated the submarine's value for them; the Americans did not realize that in submarines they had a war-winning weapon, that in an unrestricted campaign against enemy commerce they would succeed where Germany had failed once and would fail again.

For just over two hours on the morning of 7 December 1941,

Previous pages: An American submarine in action against Japanese shipping

354 Japanese aircraft rained destruction on U.S. army and navy installations on the Hawaiian island of Oahu. It was a flawlessly executed raid, bold, thorough, and wonderfully co-ordinated. Only a few of the attackers failed to return to the waiting aircraft carriers and the Japanese were cock-a-hoop. Had they not been so flushed with success they might have drawn one discomforting conclusion from an otherwise unblemished performance. It had been assumed that twenty-seven I class submarines and five midget submarines of the Japanese Sixth Fleet would deal a heavier blow than the carrier-based aircraft. The midgets were to slide into Pearl Harbor and attack the stationary American battle fleet while the full-size submarines waited outside to pick off ships making a break for the open sea. The scheme came to nothing: all five midget submarines were destroyed and the bigger boats failed lamentably in their assigned task of sealing off the harbour. It was the first of many failures.

Above: The Japanese surprise attack on Pearl Harbor, 7 December 1941. The carrier-based aircraft performed wonderfully; the submarines failed completely. Below: A Japanese midget submarine salvaged after the raid

The extent to which American submarines outclassed those of the Japanese can hardly be overstated, yet for the first few months of the war things went so badly for the Allies that there was no indication of what submarines might achieve under more favourable conditions. The fifty-five American submarines in the Pacific were divided between the Pacific Fleet at Pearl Harbor and the Asiatic Fleet based on the Philippines. The flotilla at Pearl Harbor emerged unscathed from the holocaust of 7 December and moved at once to attack shipping in Japanese waters. But while the campaign was unrestricted from the day war was declared there were not enough submarines available to mount a serious threat. The Asiatic Fleet submarines were powerless to hinder let alone stay the Japanese advance and found themselves pushed all the way back to Western Australia for a secure base. Submarines on both sides engaged at Midway

in June 1942, but that momentous battle was settled by carrier-based aircraft. The American victory at Midway was the turning point in the Pacific war, but it did not herald the appearance of submarines in a war-winning capacity. They played only a supporting role for the Americans in the savage fighting for the Solomon Islands and during this critical period, the second half of 1942, the campaign to throttle Japanese commerce had not yet got into its stride. In fact while the Solomons campaign went against them it was the Japanese who made better use of submarines, not only in strikes against U.S. warships but in getting supplies through to their beleaguered forces on Guadalcanal.

The tide of battle was now running against Japan and as the tempo quickened American submarines and submariners began to show the qualities for which they are justly famed. During 1943 Japanese shipping came under increasingly heavy attack, and these fleet-type American submarines were superlative weapons, better even than U-boats. They were of around 1,500 tons displacement, had a 10,000-mile range, and could make 20 knots on the surface and half that speed submerged. For the first part of the war their 21-inch torpedoes had a disturbing habit of running too deep, often well under the target, but this defect was now being sorted out. Far and away the greatest technical achievement in these submarines, however, was S.J. radar, with which they could locate enemy shipping at night. Since neither Japanese ships nor aircraft had radar at this stage it gave American submarines a tremendous advantage and it was exploited fully.

Left: Twenty years after the raid on Pearl Harbor this midget submarine is hoisted aboard a Japanese ship for the journey home. Below: A Japanese I class submarine, large and reliable but badly hampered by lack of radar

The tactics developed by submariners matched the technical sophistication of their boats, and for the first time a situation arose in which submarine chasers were at a disadvantage in a straightforward clash with their prey. Regardless of other factors this spelled ruin for Japan. If a convoy escort cannot attack marauding submarines with any degree of confidence then the convoy system cannot possibly defeat a determined submarine campaign. Had that been the case during the Battle of the Atlantic (or in 1917) then Britain must surely have bowed to the U-boat. The Americans became highly skilled at what they called the 'down the throat shot'. This graphic bit of slang nicely captures the spirit of American submariners and it refers to a hair-raising technique for coping with destroyers. The traditional move when picked up by asdic was to submerge quickly and deeply and hope for the best. The Americans scorned this defensive ploy and instead held their ground until the charging destroyer was at point-blank range. Then, at the last moment, they would loose a spread of torpedoes right 'down the throat'. This was a brilliant innovation and it required great coolness as well as flair, since if the destroyer were not stopped dead in its tracks the submarine must court death.

Whereas the American submarine campaign picked up speed slowly and then went on from strength to triumph, the Japanese campaign began inauspiciously, achieved its finest results in the losing struggle for the Solomons, and went steadily downhill from there. The boats themselves were slightly larger than their American counterparts, they were of roughly equivalent performance, and their torpedoes worked well from the beginning. But they lacked radar, which not only impaired their effectiveness on offence but rendered them extremely vulnerable to American anti-submarine measures, whether directed by aircraft, surface vessels, or submarines, all of which were radar-equipped. It is difficult to imagine how the Japanese could have broken out of the vicious circle resulting from their technical inferiority. Perhaps they should have acknowledged their inability to use submarines in the way they had planned—as

Left: Scores of Japanese midget submarines in dry dock at the end of the war. Above: A Kaiten suicide torpedo is launched—a gruesome tribute to Japanese courage (and American naval supremacy)

Previous pages: Japanese crewman cling to their rapidly sinking ship after being torpedoed by an American submarine. Inset: A periscope view of a Japanese ship's final moments

warships—and concentrated instead on attacking American commerce. But again it is difficult to see how they could have accomplished much in this direction. Unlike the British in the Atlantic, or the Japanese themselves in the Pacific, the Americans were not dependent upon the sea for survival. In any case when Japanese submarines posed their greatest threat they found themselves easily over-matched against the armed convoy. As the war entered its grim final stages the Japanese could think of nothing better than adapting *kamikaze* methods to submarine attack. These suicide torpedoes, called Kaitens, were directed to their target by a man inside using a periscope. It was a gruesome idea and it proved futile. Raw courage is no substitute for technical inventiveness.

In 1943 American submarines severely curtailed the Japanese war effort. In 1944 they crushed it beyond repair. The great battle of the Philippine Sea (June) and Leyte Gulf (October) marked the end of the Japanese navy as an effective force, and in both cases submarines played a major role. The first of these was the only fleet action ever fought in which submarines could claim *the* major role since they accounted for two of the three Japanese aircraft carriers sunk. Independent of these decisive battles American submarines racked up an impressive record against warships encountered on routine patrol. More calamitous from the Japanese point of view was the wholesale destruction of their merchant navy. Operating singly or sometimes in small, loosely-controlled 'wolf-packs', the American submarines were unanswerable. In 1943 they inflicted losses of between 50,000 and 230,000 tons per month. In 1944 they averaged more than 200,000 tons per month, and when the tally fell dramatically towards the end of the year it was for the simple reason that there was little left to sink.

With their merchant marine in ruins the Japanese could not possibly stave off defeat. Their lifeline to the outside world was severed. They were desperately short of food and the raw materials necessary to run an industrial economy, especially one geared to war. In modern times even the most fanatical warrior is impotent without iron to build his ships and planes, and oil to power them. It has been said that the denial of oil was in a sense 'most' crucial but there is no point in arguing degrees of absolute. As American aircraft mopped up what was left of Japanese shipping in the first half of 1945, Japan was absolutely prostrate, whether her leaders cared to admit it or not. The atomic bomb strikes against Hiroshima and Nagasaki should not be viewed as the necessary alternative to launching a bloody invasion of Japan. They were an unnecessary alternative to choking Japan into submission. For the first time in world history a nation was brought to its knees by an assault on its commerce: for the only time in its brief history the submarine was decisive as a war-winning weapon.

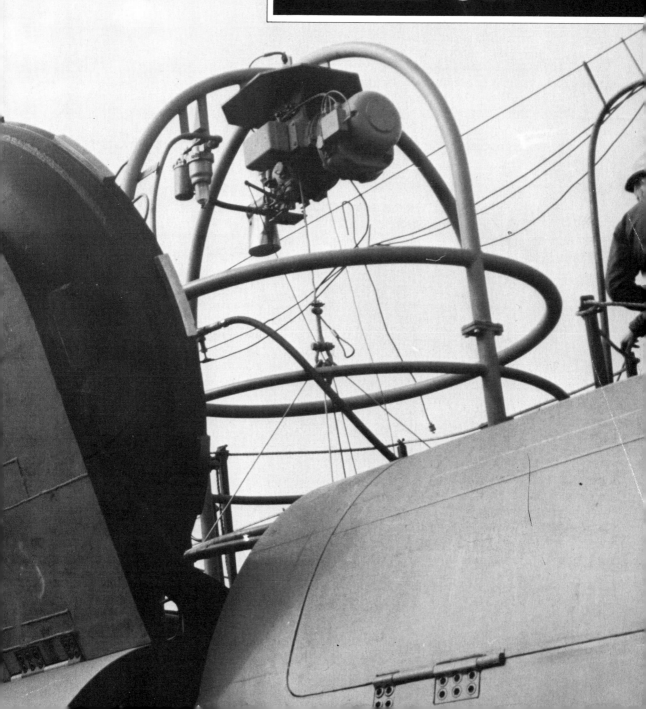

10. THE MOST FORMIDABLE WEAPON

The advent of nuclear-powered submarines in the mid-fifties revolutionized sea power. The marriage of nuclear missiles to nuclear submarines a few years later was perhaps more important even than the development of the atomic bomb itself. Not surprisingly, other post-war advances in submarine technology are easily overlooked since they are so completely overshadowed, but a few of them are important.

The thread must be picked up with the U-boats routed in the spring of 1943. They were forced to abandon the Battle of the Atlantic because they were beaten technically and tactically by the Allied counter-attack. They could no longer operate on the surface at night because they could not escape the searching eye of radar. The obvious theoretical answer was to go back to first principles and develop a true submarine boat in place of the submersible torpedo-boat, and this was what the Germans did. They concluded rightly that the anti-submarine measures ranged against them would be quite ineffective if they could somehow attack convoys at high speed while submerged. Radar would be useless and the aircraft menace removed. Asdic would be no threat to a submarine that could match a destroyer in speed.

The Germans were not only right about this but they were able to act on it. In Dr Hellmuth Walther they possessed a brilliant engineer, and since 1937 he had been experimenting with a hydrogen-peroxide engine. By 1943 he had progressed far enough to prompt official action, and Doenitz ordered a crash development programme. The Walther engine worked on the principle that hydrogen peroxide passed over a catalyst furnishes oxygen and water. The oxygen and water are fed into a combustion chamber, sprayed with fuel, and the resulting mixture burns very hot, generating steam. The addition of more water results in more steam, and this powers a turbine which in turn powers the submarine. Spectacular results were expected from this engine: it would be expensive to run but according to calculations a submerged speed of 25 knots was well within reach. The snag was, such a technological leap could not be accomplished overnight. Given the worsening situation on all fronts the Germans did well to produce four small Walther submarines by V.E. Day.

In the shorter term they pressed forward with the development of an advanced U-boat, one that sacrificed surface performance to underwater speed. This could be achieved by stream-lining the hull (something like the old French *sousmarins*) and incorporating a much larger battery. Again the reasoning was sound but defeat came before these type XXI U-boats (and a smaller version, type XXIII) were able to show their mettle. Where the Germans did manage to break new ground with a measure of success was with the schnorkel. This was a telescopic 'breathing' tube that fed air into the diesel engine and carried

off exhaust gases. A schnorkel-equipped U-boat could run submerged on its diesel engine at the same time charging its batteries. While it could do so only at a slow speed and a shallow depth this greatly reduced the chances of being picked up by radar, and it was merciful for the Allies that this development came towards the end of the war rather than at the beginning. As it was the schnorkel enabled U-boats to continue operations in home waters right to the end.

It is an intriguing though unanswerable question whether any or all of these developments had they come to fruition, say, in 1942 would have swung the war Germany's way. In any case the victorious Allies realized that the submarine of the immediate future was infinitely more potent than anything they had fought with or fought against. They wasted no time in picking up where the Germans had left off. The British were particularly active, tackling the three new fronts simultaneously. They equipped their submarines with schnorkels and began experiments with a type XXI U-boat and a Walther boat. They went further, and laid down two hydrogen-peroxide-fuelled submarines of British design. The first of these, *Explorer*, finally went into service in 1956, but while she was an excellent submarine it was her misfortune to be obsolete from birth. On 17 January 1955 the U.S.S. *Nautilus* signalled that she was underway on nuclear power, and this was not a new development in submarines but a new dimension.

The overwhelming superiority of the nuclear-powered submarine lies in its ability to travel at high speed submerged for a period of time that is in practical terms limitless. It has often been said that the *Nautilus* was the first 'true' submarine, that is, not a surface boat capable of submergence but one whose natural habitat is the world beneath the sea. All previous submarines could in a sense hold their breath for a prolonged dive, whereas the *Nautilus* was independent of the atmosphere. It is the difference between whales and fish.

The reason why the nuclear submarine can 'live' underwater is that a nuclear reactor requires no oxygen. A controlled nuclear reaction generates tremendous heat, which turns water into steam for running turbines. The nuclear power is also harnessed to turbo-generators in order to provide electricity. There is, of course, a need for oxygen to breathe, but this is easily stored and carefully purified. Since the only realistic limitation on the submarine's endurance is the endurance of its crew, no effort is spared to make living conditions supportable, even pleasant. Nuclear submarines vary in size between the large and the enormous, and compared with earlier submarines the crews' quarters are spacious and luxuriously appointed. A ship that spends all its time under water is constantly at risk, and even minor faults or errors of judgement are apt to be fatal, just as they are apt to be with aeroplanes. Nuclear submarines are 'safe', but they are not infallibly so, and their history has not been unmarred by tragedy. In April 1963 the *Thresher* disappeared with complete loss of life some 200 miles out from Boston in deep water; five years later another nuclear submarine, U.S.S. *Scorpion*, was lost in mid-Atlantic.

The *Nautilus* was an immediate, unqualified success, and the Americans were quick to exploit their technological breakthrough. During the late 1950s many more of these craft went into service, most of them, like *Nautilus*, designated 'attack' submarines. They varied between three and four thousand tons displacement (roughly twice the size of American fleet submarines of the Second World War) and had an underwater cruising speed of 20–25 knots. These submarines quickly smashed all existing records for performance. In 1958 *Nautilus* made the journey from the Pacific to Great Britain by the short polar route. On 10 May 1960 U.S.S. *Triton* completed a round the world jaunt following Magellan's route of more than four centuries before—totally submerged. One can only speculate as to how devastating such warships would be in action since, mercifully, they have not been put to the test. War games, however, if they can never provide unanswerable proof at least offer a wealth of evidence. The summer before *Triton*'s epic voyage a combined NATO fleet enacted full-dress battle in the Mediterranean. Hostilities closed after the attack submarine *Skipjack* 'sank' every aircraft carrier involved in the exercises.

Right top: The first nuclear-powered submarine, U.S.S. *Nautilus*, slips into the Thames River in Connecticut, after being christened by America's First Lady, Mamie Eisenhower. This was 21 January 1957. A year later, almost to the day, she was 'underway on nuclear power'

Right below: U.S.S. *Triton*, which circled the world submerged in 1960. Her epic voyage was proof that the nuclear submarine enjoyed a range of action that was virtually limitless

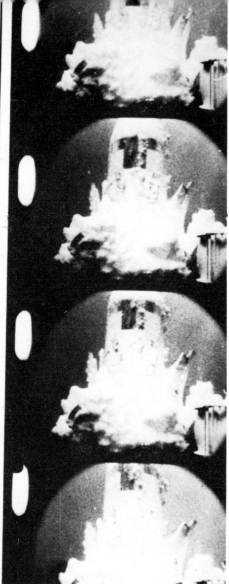

Even this pales by comparison with the Polaris programme. The idea of using submarines as launching pads for rockets was not new. Before *Nautilus* the Americans had adapted some conventional submarines to carry a single short-range Regulus missile. One of the early nuclear submarines, the *Halibut*, was equipped with several of these missiles. But in both cases they could be fired only from the surface, a great handicap. On 20 July 1960 U.S.S. *George Washington* fired a Polaris ballistic missile from a submerged position, and from that point it can safely be said that the submarine exceeded the most extravagant predictions ever made for it. It was no longer primarily concerned with sea power but with overall military power. It could be seen as the most potent weapon in the nuclear arsenal or as the ultimate deterrent to nuclear war or both.

Right: U.S.S. *George Washington*, the first nuclear-powered submarine to launch a Polaris missile when submerged (July 1960)

Right: U.S.S. *George Washington*, the first nuclear-powered submarine to launch a Polaris missile when submerged (July 1960)

The obvious difference between missile-equipped submarines and any other is that their threat is not limited to, or even directed towards, maritime traffic, naval or commercial. The A-3 Polaris missile, with which most of the forty-one American Polaris submarines were equipped by the early 1970s, has a range of 2,800 miles. Approximately twenty of these submarines are constantly on patrol, undetected by any potential enemy. Each carries sixteen missiles, and within minutes of the order going out all these lethal devices would be hurtling towards predetermined targets. Because the whereabouts of these submarines is unknown it would be impossible to knock them out in a pre-emptive strike. Hence their description as a second-strike delivery system. In theory they make nuclear attack unthinkable since the instigator of it would know for certain that he was signing his own death-warrant. Even were

Left: As the Duke of Edinburgh (third from left on raised platform) presses a switch the first section of H.M.S. *Dreadnought* is drawn on to the slipway. The keel of Britain's first nuclear submarine was laid at Barrow-in-Furness in June 1959. Below left: H.M.S. *Resolution,* launched in September 1966. Right and below: Two views of the *Dreadnought* underway

he to annihilate his victim at one blow he must in turn
perish brief moments later.

As with the atomic and hydrogen bombs, the American
monopoly of nuclear submarines was short-lived. First the
British, then the Russians, and finally the French moved into
the new field. H.M.S. *Dreadnought*, similar to the Skipjack
class, entered service in the early 1960s, while the first British
Polaris submarine was laid down in 1964 and accepted for
service in 1967. By the early 1970s the Royal Navy possessed
thirty-five submarines in all, including four Polaris and seven
torpedo-armed nuclear fleet submarines. While some naval
experts regard this as insufficient (deploring in particular the
decision not to build a fifth Polaris) it is nevertheless an
impressive striking force. The French embarked on missile-
equipped nuclear submarines in the mid-sixties, and the first

of four, the *Redoutable*, was operational in 1971. But since neither Britain nor France is a military rival of the United States it is the development of nuclear submarines by the Soviet Union that is of moment. The Russian navy grew to immense proportions during the 1960s, and despite making a late start in nuclear submarines it very rapidly closed the gap with the U.S. navy. According to the most recent figures (1973) the Russians possess ninety-five nuclear-powered submarines, twenty-five of them equipped with ballistic missiles. They also have by far the largest flotilla of diesel-powered submarines— more than 300—and some of these also carry missiles.

It does not follow from this that American submarines are no longer pre-eminent. Thirty-one of the forty-one Polaris submarines are of the advanced Lafayette class (7,500 tons) and their A-3 Polaris missiles are steadily being replaced by Poseidon missiles of similar range but twice the payload. The fifty-five nuclear fleet (or attack) submarines are to be augmented by twenty more. The first of a new class of Trident submarines, which will carry missiles with a 6,000-mile range, should be completed by 1978. The Russians are less forthcoming about their current achievements and future plans, but it is a moot point whether their drive for naval supremacy will be rewarded with success.

Any history of submarines must end inconclusively because their development is an ongoing thing. Our position today is not dissimilar to that of naval theorists in the years leading up to the First World War. It was generally accepted that the submarine must somehow affect traditional concepts of sea power but there was, with very few exceptions, only a hazy idea of what that effect would be. After all they were grappling with an untested weapon. At present it is easy enough to say that the missile-carrying nuclear submarine has such awesome power that war between those who possess it is fantastical. It is to be hoped that this is so, and we shall never find out whether nuclear warface is as conclusive as we suspect it is, and whether the Polaris-type submarine is as unanswerable as it appears. We take comfort from nuclear stalemate, and barring madness or catastrophic blunder stalemate brings an uneasy security. It is remotely conceivable that great powers could engage in war without resorting to nuclear weapons, in which case 'ordinary' nuclear submarines would certainly dominate naval hostilities. Then again it is possible that some comprehensive defence system will be employed against the ballistic missile. But it is obvious that such a defence would have to be not only flawless but known to be flawless, and in the foreseeable future this is unlikely to say the least. The advantage rests with the offence, and the deterrence lies in the certainty of massive retaliation. For all its destructive power the modern submarine may turn out to be the great peace-keeper.